MANAGEMENT 101

What They Should Have Told You

I0116864

JOHN BALESTRIERI

CHAPTERS

INTRODUCTION

So, you want to be in management. Management is a noble pursuit that sometimes stretches, sometimes frustrates, and many times rewards, but ultimately helps an individual grow more than any other pursuit outside of marriage and parenthood.

Yes, there is a difference between management and leadership. The ideal combination of both yields a terrific and valuable employee that can be a spark plug for any company or organization. Who would not want to follow someone who could handle the day-to-day issues of employees, projects, and deadlines while at the same time be able to point the way to something higher and more achievable exclaiming to their subordinates either in voice or action, "follow me men (and women)" to that next level?

However, what is missing in all of this is the training, mentoring, and the basic understanding of management. Unfortunately, what they should have told you in undergraduate or graduate school is not discovered until you're actually on the job. To be fair, it may be a challenge for those in academia to address these gaps if they are somewhat removed from the front lines of the management world.

How many times have you seen the most technical person or most senior person in your work area promoted to a management position who was not ready nor possessed the needed qualities and training for the job? In these situations, the result can look and feel like the tallest pigmy was chosen when in reality the selecting official never identified the person's giftedness and abilities and then aligned those to the management duties that were needed for the position.

It is an accepted belief that to earn more money in the workplace, one has to enter into management since those positions pay more than non-management positions. We still have a hard time in the American business culture differentiating between the value of an effective non-management employee and a manager. The employee knows this as well. Thus, he/she realizes, that if they want to climb to the next level then they have to make the move to management to receive the financial compensation they are looking for. From the individual's standpoint, even if they are the right person for the job, they may have not been groomed and instructed in the fundamentals of "Management 101" that would have helped them to be successful. Then, there are those who are already in management who could benefit from some coaching and insight in order to become a better manager. This book seeks to address these two dilemmas. Specifically, it was written to help those who aspire to be in management or who are currently in management and desire to be more successful. Welcome to *Management 101: What They Should Have Told You!*

CHAPTER 1

ORGANIZATIONAL DESIGN

I would like to start things off with how a company or organization is designed. This helps to provide a preliminary understanding of where you as an employee fit, which is very important in order to function within its makeup. So what is organizational design? Basically, it is the way an organization is structured and operates. The design of any organizational model can be a strong indicator to predict how well it can:

1. Efficiently operate

2. Control costs

3. Provide customer service

4. Improve throughput times

5. Embrace change

6. **Motivate its employees**

7. **Create and sustain a positive work culture**

8. **Achieve profitability**

9. **Allow for growth of its business**

How well is your company or organization achieving any of these goals with its current model? Whatever your answer is to this question is a direct reflection of how well it is designed. When any of the nine indicators listed above are lagging, you can be certain that the organizational design is the cause. Thus, find the cause, and you can find the cure and potentially improve any flawed area of the design.

Organizational Structures

Most organizational structures departmentalize the workforce and other resources by either functions or products. Functional organizations are segmented by key functions such as finance, marketing, or manufacturing and placed into their own department. These respective departments can contain divisions of their own. See Table 1. In contrast, companies that employ what is called a product or divisional structure, break the organization down into semiautonomous units and profit centers based on activities or "projects" such as: products, customers, or geographic location. Each unit operates as a separate business regardless of the project used to segment the company. See Table 2. Then we have matrix management, which combines both the functional and product departmentalization in a dual reporting

TABLE 1: FUNCTIONAL ORGANIZATIONAL STRUCTURE

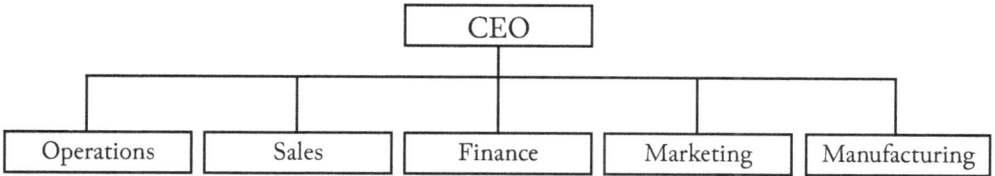

```
                           CEO

Operations    Sales    Finance    Marketing    Manufacturing
```

TABLE 2: PRODUCT/DIVISIONAL ORGANIZATIONAL STRUCTURE

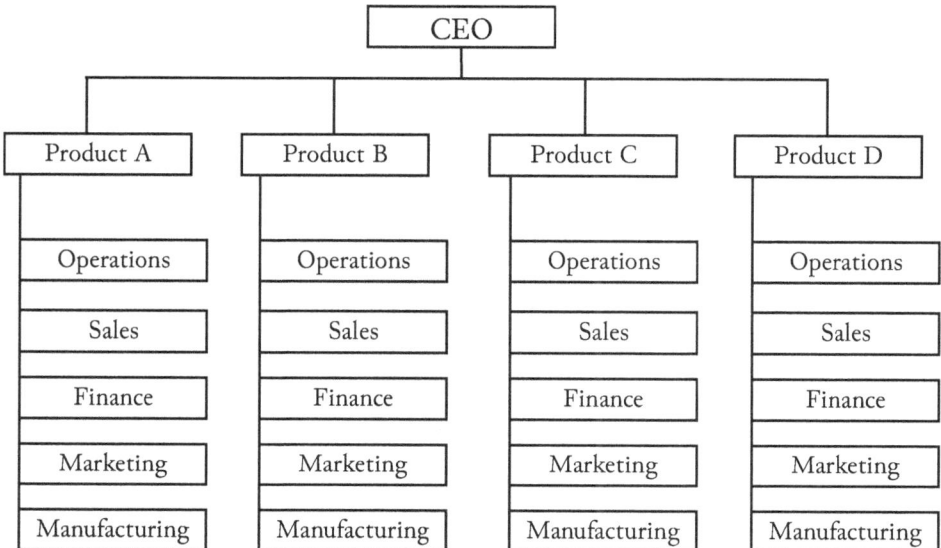

```
                              CEO

   Product A        Product B        Product C        Product D

  Operations       Operations       Operations       Operations

    Sales            Sales            Sales            Sales

   Finance          Finance          Finance          Finance

  Marketing        Marketing        Marketing        Marketing

 Manufacturing    Manufacturing    Manufacturing    Manufacturing
```

system.[1] Thus, there are a number of organizational design models, but in this book I will focus on bureaucratic management and matrix management. These specific models do lean toward larger establishments, but at some point in your professional career, you will work either in or with these two types of organizations. Understanding how they operate will allow you to succeed and even incorporate some nuances into your current system. Notwithstanding, you will definitely be able to recognize how the federal and state governments are set up to operate and why they struggle.

Bureaucratic Management

Bureaucracy. That word automatically brings negative connotations of red tape, numerous layers of management, and inefficiency. However, the bureaucratic theory of management was developed by Maximillian Weber, a German sociologist and political economist. He is considered one of the three founders of sociology along with Karl Marx and Emile Durkheim.[2] Around the beginning of the 20th century, it is maintained that he was the first to coin the word "bureaucracy" and describe its meaning. Weber felt that in a large organization, the bureaucratic method of management was essential for it to run effectively. Consequently, if you are in a large organization where change is unanticipated, then it is probably using Weber's organizational model of bureaucracy to run things. In particular, that would be the government, military, colleges and universities, and large-sized businesses.

There are six bureaucratic management principles as defined by Weber.[3] They are:

1. Division of Labor by Specialization

Each department or division office has a specific sphere and defined area of expertise and responsibility. This is the division of labor that the organization benefits from as the work is defined and shared. Work tasks/duties are distributed on the basis of individual competencies and functional specialization that they focus on and do not deviate from. Every employee knows their place and function in the organization, and no work gaps exist.

2. Managerial Hierarchy

The basic feature of a bureaucratic organization is the hierarchy of positions that exist in the organization. Hierarchy is a system of ranking various positions in descending scale from the top of the organization, with its authority, all the way to the bottom of the organization to include managers who are given authority and responsibility for their work area and assigned staff. Departments or divisions also follow the principle of hierarchy that each lower office is subject to control, supervision, and communication by the next higher office. They can possess similar levels of authority but within their own respective focus of expertise.

3. Qualification-based Selection

Employees must meet the technical requirements of the position to be selected along with their level of competency. They will then be compensated based on that particular position they are to encumber. The merit system is the basis of selection that is considered objective and unbiased vice subjective with personal preferences. For example, the federal and state governments tout the merit system as its way of hiring and promoting its workforce to ensure fairness is provided.

Unfortunately, that system is not uncorrupted and many times deviates from the original intent when hiring managers show bias even though an appearance of objectivity is demonstrated.

4. Rules and Official Policy

The establishment of and heavy reliance on strict rules and official policy is a key element of the bureaucratic organization. It is heavily relied upon to ensure stability and order is maintained. Expectations and outcomes are clearly understood by the employees as a result. It is a guide for the workforce to follow that fosters compliance more than creativity. When overdone, this leads to the "red tape" label so often used in a bureaucracy and why change is so hard to achieve. When a new rule or policy is needed, the issue is submitted to the upward level of managerial hierarchy to become permanent guidance.

5. Impersonal Relationships

The bureaucratic organization was designed to promote fairness and impartiality among its employees and customers that allows for unbiased decision-making by those in authority. Relationships are restricted to a professional manner mainly due to the previous four management principles discussed. This in turn evokes a perception of being impersonal from both the employees' and customers' perspective. In sacrificing those relationships, the positive qualities and beneficial outcomes of them are lost. From Max Weber's time until now, the importance of relationships has become more evident in the success of a company or organization. No employee wants to be thought of as just a number, or as I often refer to it, "a bullet inserted into the chamber of a gun that is discarded by management once it has been fired." Specifically, employees can easily feel disconnected from the organization when relationships are impersonal, and they do not feel they have a voice. I will discuss the importance of employee relationships more in Chapter 8, "Understanding and Handling Employee Turnover."

6. Career Inclination

As mentioned in qualification-based selection, employees are selected based on their level of technical ability and competency for the job they will be hired into. In turn, they can look to build their career and possess long-time employment within the bureaucratic organization. After a probationary period, they experience a sense of job security due to the protection the organization provides with all of the rules and official policies it is supposed to embrace. To be frank, if it is hard to invoke change within a bureaucratic organization then similarly, it is expected to be just as difficult to remove an employee. Just ask the federal government!

Do any of these principles look or sound familiar? Yeah, I thought so. At some point in your career, you may have been frustrated with the way things were running in your company or organization. You then wondered, "How in the world did this structure I am working in ever come about?" It may have felt inefficient and seemed hard to get things done in order to accomplish a certain task/project, influence change, or see process improvements occur. Well, you have Max Weber to thank as you were probably in a bureaucratic run organization, which by the way, is a classic model of organization design still employed today even though many of Weber's writings have been discredited. However, let us consider the advantages and disadvantages of the bureaucratic management design.

Advantages:

Some of the positive aspects of a bureaucratic organization are[4]:

1. All of its employees understand the rules and official policies.

2. Employees clearly know their job functions.

3. Employees are selected via merit, based on their technical ability and competency.

4. The managerial hierarchy is understood by all.

5. How the organization functions and responds in scenarios is understood by all.

Disadvantages:

Some of the negative aspects of a bureaucratic organization are[4]:

1. Many hierarchical layers.

2. High cost to run.

3. Slower decision-making.

4. Resistant to change.

5. Impersonal nature it fosters.

The bureaucratic organization's resistance to change is a killer to many companies and organizations. In Chapter 7, "Change Management," we will discuss change management and why many times it is difficult to enact in an organization. *What they should have told you in undergraduate or graduate school is that the type of organization design you are a part of will determine how easy or hard change can be to implement.* You see, employees in any organization tend to become accustomed to how it operates. People inherently like predictability. In the case of the bureaucratic organizational design, the system becomes so ingrained within the psyche of its employees that they will resist both strategic change throughout the organization and operational change within their department or work unit to reorganize, improve processes, etc., if it is ever attempted.

The impersonal nature of relationships is very important to note. It results in employees becoming less loyal to the organization due to feeling distanced and as if they have no voice or influence in the organization.

Overall, these disadvantages lead to inefficiency. Thus, employees can be demotivated in the long run. Ask any government employee about this as their system is set up to be a sort of demotivation to do more, make change, or improve processes. "What's in it for me if I do this extra task?" becomes the question. In other words, "What's my motivation?" Have you ever seen the movie *Office Space* and the famous interview scene? In this particular scene, the lead character Peter, played by Ron Livingston, responds to the efficiency experts, "the Bobs," in the same manner. He says the classic line, "So where's the motivation?"[5] when it comes to wanting to do more for the company. Just type "Office Space Interview Scene" into your browser and watch the two-minute video clip. It is telling.

Matrix Management

New concepts of organizational design began to surface a few decades after the Max Weber bureaucracy model. One such concept mentioned earlier is matrix management. It is a style of organizational design that was first introduced around the late 1940s but became more accepted and mainstream with larger companies by the 1970s.[4] Matrix management combines both the functional and product departmentalization in a dual reporting system. Unlike the strictness of the bureaucratic organization design, which functions by authority and control, matrix management was designed to introduce more flexibility with less managerial hierarchy in contrast. With less managerial hierarchy, there are also fewer layers of decision-making required.

When running a large organization, the need for creativity and the ability to adapt became paramount following the post-World War era. Thus, matrix management was looking to counter the negatives of the traditional design models, like the bureaucratic model, while still maintaining a level of control. Keep in mind, the impetus for change is usually driven by some causal affect. Specifically, competition will usually force a business to make adjustments to its design structure when it realizes it is falling behind or will fall behind its rival(s).

The key distinction of the matrix management organizational design is the dual reporting relationships it possesses which differs from the norm in traditional management structures.[5] Employees report to two managers, regardless of the functional department or division they are primarily hired into. This concept was designed to manage cross-functional business groups and may be on a long-term basis or a short-term/temporary basis similar to a "work cell" created to complete a project or solve a particular problem. Accordingly, this model can be used for cross-functional project teams as well. See Table 3 for an example of cross-functional groups and its products and/ or services. Simply substitute Project A in the left hand column for Product A/Service A and so on.

I personally have been a part of a matrix management model when working for a large organization that had locations throughout the United States and overseas. We had functional managers and operational managers. The employees administratively belonged to their functional manager who was located at a higher headquarters, but worked for and primarily reported to their operational manager who they physically reported to on a daily basis. However, my organization's "product" was our customers who resided in many geographic locations (see the left hand column), which is another use of matrix management. See Table 4 on the next page.

TABLE 3: CROSS-FUNCTIONAL GROUPS AND ITS PRODUCTS OR SERVICES IT DELIVERS

	OPERATIONS	SALES	FINANCE	MARKETING	MANUFACTURING
PRODUCT A/SERVICE A					
PRODUCT B/SERVICE B					
PRODUCT C/SERVICE C					
PRODUCT D/SERVICE D					

TABLE 4: CROSS-FUNCTIONAL GROUPS AND GEOGRAPHICAL LOCATION

	OPERATIONS	SALES	FINANCE	MARKETING	MANUFACTURING
NORFOLK, VA					
SAN DIEGO, CA					
HONOLULU, HI					
NAPLES, ITALY					

Advantages

As I stated earlier, matrix management was designed to introduce more flexibility with less managerial hierarchy into a large organization that tends to operate in a faster-paced style or tempo. As Mark Twain said, "Too much of anything is bad." As such, too much management is definitely bad for any organization. Therefore, when layers of management are reduced, as what occurs in matrix management models, the organization becomes "flatter" and communication increases. This results in information being exchanged and cooperation increasing. Thus, change can happen and much faster in a matrix management organization than in a traditional management model. However, this is predicated on having managers who are themselves flexible and open to change and innovation. They adjust when necessary and have their employees follow suit, i.e. lead by example. It becomes contagious, and employees see the fruits of their labor on a regular basis, which is a big motivator. Finally, a matrix management model consists of a workforce that is primarily made up of white-collar professionals who possess different skill sets in order to take advantage of their collective abilities. Soft skills such as communication in particular, cannot be underestimated.

Disadvantages

Even though the advantages seem appealing in making a large organization work better, it does have its downfalls. First, the cost can be high to keep this management model operating with its dual reporting relationships and administrative overhead. Second, it can be very confusing to initially introduce this management model to managers and employees and for them to accept it when coming from a traditional management concept. Third, I have discovered that loyalties tend to be tested as an employee who administratively belongs to their functional manager has a tendency to become allied to their operational manager in whom they physically report to on a daily basis. This becomes even more of an issue when that employee is geographically distanced from their functional manager as well. In the government or military system for example, the chain of command is very important to the workforce because it helps them clarify roles. The matrix management model causes unease with its employees because they feel there is no clear chain of command and with that, the person to whom they can truly call "the boss." Consequently, many times the employee can find himself or herself in the middle of being given two different sets of directions to follow. Finally, any "temporary" cells created to accomplish a project or solve a problem, with the intent of returning the employees to their functional group, tend to prolong and extend the employee's duration. As those who can attest in larger organizations, the words "short-term" and "temporary" many times turn into "long-term" and "permanent." This drives up costs and can lead to added stress for the other employees in that individual's work unit who have to cover the gap created by the time extension of the term or temporary assignment.

Technology and Agility

Regardless of its design, structure is needed for any organization and its operations to function. The problem arising in today's marketplace is that technology is outpacing large organizations' ability to change and adjust. With technology comes new competitors who do not necessarily have to start with the entrenched bureaucracy. Therefore, it has the ability to innovate more rapidly and bring its product(s) to market faster. You may have heard the phrase, "It is much easier to turn a PT boat than a battleship." There is a lot of truth in that saying. Agility will become an often-used buzzword, if it hasn't already, for larger companies to possess longevity. Just ask Kmart, Sears, J.C. Penney, etc. who once dominated in the retail space but have lost market share over the last three decades. Everyone is looking for a new product or niche, but what they should be looking for are ways to adjust their organization to meet the next business wave cycle. Breaking the larger organization down into more manageable and functional units, in order to allow it to refocus on what business platforms it wants to be successful, is the key to the future.

General Electric Company under Jack Welch did just that. It was revolutionary for a big company to embark on this type of endeavor, but it took someone who wanted to "break it" in order to make it better. I'll say it more than once in this book that it all starts and ends with leadership. The leader just has to have the vision to make the change and the temerity to see it through. This is true for both the private and public sectors.

CHAPTER 2

EVERYONE WANTS TO BE IN A GANG

Now that is a chapter title you never thought would be in a book on management. But it is truer than you may think and relates to identity. As I have grown older and had to interact with different groups of people in the business world, it seems to be more prevalent when someone is a part of a reticent corporate culture.

You were probably first exposed to this gang concept early on in junior high or high school. You had your school name, mascot, team jersey, school logo, cheerleaders, prep rallies, etc. But then, there was the college football season in the fall, and this is where it magnified to the point that even the isolated curmudgeon seemed to morph into an extravert taking on an ENFP Myers-Briggs Type personality profile.

Sense of Identity

I grew up in western Pennsylvania and when the University of Pittsburgh (PITT) would play Penn State University in football each year, the PITT fans would come out and identify themselves by wearing their garb and rooting their Panthers on hoping for an upset over the more established Nittany Lions. Hence, by being from western PA, many folks identified with Pittsburgh and the PITT brand. Penn State was located in the middle of Pennsylvania and yes, to be fair, there were some western PA folks who rooted for them. We all make mistakes in life. I digress. PITT had a deep history in college football, winning many championships over the years, but only one in recent memory which was in 1976. Penn State was a perennial powerhouse and had won a couple of championships beyond 1976 and was able to recruit better talent from all over the country to include some athletes from PITT's backyard of western PA. So, it became more of a David versus Goliath match with PITT pulling out a win once every few years. As I witnessed this identification of the association with PITT, I also saw the elements that went into it. To me, it appeared that there were many of the same characteristics I saw evident in such things that caused people to choose sides during the "cola wars" of the 70s and 80s, the Ford and Chevrolet truck television campaigns during the same time frame, the Army/Navy/Air Force/Marine Corps quarrels, any high school or college rivalries. It goes on and on. I would hear people vehemently and proudly proclaim things like, "I'm a Marine (and once a Marine always a Marine), I'm a Ford man, a New Yorker, a Texan, a Sicilian. I'm a Buckeye, a Wolverine, a Bruin, a Packer Backer, a Cowboys fan, a Lakers fan, a Red Sox fan. I'm a Catholic, a Baptist, a Buddhist. I'm a Democrat, a Republican, a Libertarian." Many even have the bumper sticker, T-shirt, commercialized desk item, or tattoo to show for it. It seems that people align themselves with a faction to allow them to be part of something bigger than themselves. From this alignment they gain a sense of community with fellow believers who also hold the same kind of fundamental and mutual belief. It provides them a sense of identity and even self-esteem. As part of the "gang," they are imprinted like a real tattoo, whether real or metaphorical. Notwithstanding, in all the companies and organizations I have worked for or with, many times I see a type of "work gang" association come about within its members.

In prison, it seems that the inmates align themselves with a gang inside the facility for self-preservation and protection, all the while hoping to gain some advantage over the rest of the population. By comparison, I have seen this occur for some of the same reasons in many companies or organizations. Those who align with certain groups sometimes get the breaks of advancement, special consideration, or privileges. *What they should have told you in undergraduate or graduate school is that the work gang is political, and the power realized from the pack can many times overwhelm those who remain neutral as individuals.* When exclusive assignments are given or budget reductions made, those aligned to their work gang try to reap the benefits of that affiliation.

While working with the Department of Defense, I used to see this work gang mentality prevalent all of the time, and it used to drive me crazy! I would see it used in meetings to gain a consensus even when the facts supported a different conclusion. I would hear it from those who were retired military who somehow found their way into becoming a civilian manager. Likewise, I would see it in the prejudices used to hire individuals from an organization in which some of the hiring panel were previously associated. Many times, the candidate(s) hired did not possess the skill set and abilities that were truly required of the position they were going to assume. I used to wonder, "Why can't people stand on their own merits and allow that to be their brand?" That of course is a naïve and unadulterated way of thinking. How dare the party in question have to solely rely upon themselves and their performance abilities without attaining a political edge they believed they needed over their co-workers within the company?

You know it's bad when an individual is not even able to break into a company through the established hiring process. I have known of several organizations in which an outside person would rarely be hired simply because of the parochial nature in its employment practices, even though they were legally obligated to comply with federal law. The company may have a policy of being open in its hiring, but it was not enforced. Their mentality was that if a person did not begin their career with that company or organization then no "outsider" would be permitted to enter, especially later on during their mid-career or higher level. It became the "who do you know there" if you ever had a chance to become part of the rank-in-file at the entry level. This hiring practice was not isolated regionally as I saw this occur in western Pennsylvania where I grew up, in Italy where I have lived, and in various workplaces on both the East and West Coast.

The First Introduction to the Work Gang

I remember early in my career it was very apparent and well-known that the human resources (HR) and financial departments ran the place. The HR director and financial director used their influence to ensure things went a certain way, and no one dared to cross them. Of course, many directors attempted to get on their good side, but were not able to get into that work gang. It was not until those two personalities moved on due to retirement that things changed. I do not believe they were bad people, just very draconian in their ways when it came to supporting or not supporting other departments. They influenced operations and policy by wielding the power they carried within their gang. They were in essence, the power behind the throne. The question to ask is, "How did this gang come about?" Glad you asked. The senior manager at our workplace encumbered their position for only two to three years due to the organization's rotational policy expected of its executive level personnel. Thus, the next person to rotate into that key position had to rely on those two tenured voices who now had his/her ear on a continual basis. The senior person defaulted to the work gang's advice and guidance. So, when that leadership head departed, the cycle started all over again.

Corporate Culture vs. Subculture

Keep in mind that a work gang does not necessarily represent the overall culture of the organization. It is usually a subculture that exists within. Specifically, a strong corporate culture will help reduce or eliminate subcultures, especially when it is drilled into its managers as the way it will conduct itself and be held accountable. A weak or reticent corporate culture will breed subcultures. Hence, the work gang mentality and the problems that ensue. No company would ever advertise its culture or state as their hiring incentive, "We have an exclusive bunch of self-serving yahoos that get special advantages over the rest of the workforce. Would you like to come work for us but be relegated to the "have nots" group?"

When selecting an organization to work for, it is helpful to see if (and how strong) the subculture mentality is, if possible. Many times, you will not know this until you are actually working at the company.

However, these entities can acquire a reputation that can be uncovered by some simple networking and asking a few questions. Some questions that could help disclose if a work gang exists: "Are there employee surveys (with rankings) that could help provide a glimpse into the culture or subculture? What is expected of those who work there? What are the inherent politics like? Who really runs things internally? How do managers get along with one another?" So what should you do when you first enter a new company or organization? Do you find and align yourself with a "work gang," or do you remain neutral and be perceived as an outsider?

I remember one particular organization that recruited me many years ago. I flew back for the interview, and they truly wanted me to be a part of their team. After I initially accepted their offer, I somehow stumbled onto the survey rankings of this organization, as determined by its employees. It was not good. The rankings placed them in the bottom 20% of the overall survey for places to work. Yikes! I kept that statistic in the back of my mind as I departed my old place of employment for this new one. My dilemma was that I not only would be taking a new management position, I was also moving cross-country for personal reasons. So, my motivations were more than just the promotion and increased pay I would be receiving. I really wanted it to work out despite the warning sign I was given. However, once there I recognized how unhealthy the subculture was in their upper management and how vindictive and ugly they treated their employees. I immediately flashed back to the survey results I read a few months prior. To make matters worse, the department secretary who was deliberately leaving for an outside position concernedly said to someone about me upon my arrival the first day in the office, "Does he understand what he is getting into here?" That was another foreboding sign. In retrospect, I should have run for the doors. After a while though, the powers that be saw that I would not join their work gang. In my new management position, I tried to remain neutral, but that did not last long. I had to make a choice to either join the gang or suffer the consequences. My issue was that I possessed what I felt was a healthy and professional viewpoint of what I believed leadership was and how management should treat its employees. I tried to protect the employees who worked for me, but that backfired after I realized that a couple of them had their own little gang that could be just as ugly as the senior leadership. This is what I inherited as the new manager. Let's be honest, toxicity breads toxicity in any company or organization. So looking back, it was not surprising to see how upper management affected the whole organization like a virus. These employees were mirroring upper management's bad behavior. As I often say, "It all starts with leadership." Everything begins with those in charge and flows downhill from there. It will cascade throughout the organization, both good and bad. It was not long before I had to make the decision to move on from there since the only way for things in a culture like that to change is if the senior management departs and new personnel replaces them. That can take years with no guarantee of a better future, and hope in itself is not a strategy to be relied upon. Consequently, the last thing you want to hear running in the back of your mind are the lyrics to The Who song, "Won't Be Fooled Again" that has the phrase, "Meet the new boss, same as the old boss."

Bottom line, a strong corporate culture can positively drive everything to include the minimizing of a subculture or gang mentality. The healthier the overall culture is, the higher the morale of the workforce, the higher the productivity level, and the less employee turnover occurs. Employees will feel emotionally safe and consequently, a greater trust will be established on all fronts. If you are in a leadership position, present a culture that reduces or eliminates the gang mentality subculture and the need for anyone to be in a work gang. If you inherit a small work gang as a result becoming a manager, look to disestablish it systematically when the opportunity presents itself. This can be accomplished through internal reorganizations, moving people onto other projects, and having candid discussions with the employees in lead positions of those area(s) stating what you observe and the effects it is having.

Many times the solution to a work gang is to bring in a new manager into that work area. Let me give you an example. Later in my career, I was brought into a key leadership/management position, being hired from the outside of the organization. I now had several division managers reporting to me. After a while, I recognized my one division manager had a couple of favorite employees whom she empowered and would often even have lunch with them in her office. She kept the rest of her employees in the dark with minimal training and job assignments. Hence, many of her talented employees were stifled, and it created a schism. The gang mentality subculture was definitely present within my department. It existed with these few individuals who were part of the inner circle of that one manager and everyone else in her division was more or less on the outside looking in. The gang members felt elite and as though they were privileged and protected by their manager. The truth was, they were. From my past managerial experience, I knew I had to break this subculture. I learned that if I did not address this, it would come back to bite me. I began by asking questions of this division manager regarding growth opportunities for her employees, work assignments, etc. I also made sure I was part of the hiring panel for any new vacancies to be filled in that division. I slowly became more intrusive. Fortunately, that division manager decided to retire in less than a year of my tenure which allowed me to hire an outside candidate who I knew would bring an unbiased attitude to the position. In my first face-to-face sit-down with that newly hired division manager, I was very frank and gave clear direction to destroy this gang attitude, level the playing field within the division, and empower/value all of the employees under their new supervision. This began to happen, and the work gang subculture was dismantled. One thing was positively certain, the other employees in that division saw the changes occur, and it renewed their trust and hope in management and the organization. Yes, people are watching what you do and how you act as a manager. Interestingly, the employees in the gang tried to hold on and even attempted to recruit the new division manager to be their new gang leader but to no avail. Overall, it took some time and a few confrontations but the gang eventually dissolved, and the playing field leveled out. Morale improved, and the remaining gang members either got on board with the new way of doing business in the division or moved on.

If a work gang subculture is going to exist in your company or organization, then everyone has to be in it, and it has to be healthy. Your ethos has to be "for the good of the company and for the people it employs." Then, the identity that eventually evolves is one that spotlights the positive attitudes and abilities the employees already possess. This type of work culture will be able to take on most anything thrown its way. Consequently, you as the manager and leader, will be recognized for being a team builder.

CHAPTER 3

DON'T LOSE YOUR MESSAGING

Messaging. This may be one of the most overlooked topics of being a manager. When you are a new manager, losing your messaging is not so much of a problem as compared to being in a company or organization for some time managing the same staff of employees. Your employees will eventually understand your overall management style, but losing your messaging can easily occur over time when you are routinely caught up in the day-to-day activities of your regular job.

Internal Messaging

Let us first talk about being a newly hired manager from the outside or maybe you have been promoted to a management position in a new work area in the same company. In any case, when you assume the role of a manager, you have the opportunity to set the tone with respect to your style, theme, and expectations that includes the messaging that you want to get across to your staff. That messaging usually comes down to a one-liner. Thus, if your staff had to answer the question, "What is your boss about?" what would you want them to say in one sentence? The reality is that whatever they would say in response to that question is what your message to them has been, period. Therefore, the time to establish yourself is when you begin your new management assignment. Do not wait a long time to do this. You will have to be proactive and demonstrate to your staff, leading by example on this one. It cannot solely be one email or just a slogan. Furthermore, if things begin to bug you about your staff, it is probably because you have expectations and an overarching theme that has not been effectively communicated. This can be frustrating as a manager when you know how things should be run but see it going awry. For example, if professionalism is important to you, then your staff needs to see this in how you conduct yourself in the office. If it is on keeping your word to a customer or peer, then you need to demonstrate that with follow-up communication so your staff sees this occurring. If it is minimizing staff travel by using teleconferencing to be in the office more, then you need to put out a clear policy on the legitimate need to travel somewhere on the company's dime, and follow it yourself. Whatever the issue you want to communicate to your staff, you explain what you expect of them and that this is how you will personally operate. Then your staff will clearly know what your messaging is, such as, "My manager expects us to conduct ourselves ethically," or "My manager expects us to travel less so we can be in the office more." Another example would be if you run a tight ship that includes:

- Starting and ending meetings on time

- Expecting work assignments to be finished on time with high quality

- Delivering presentations in a professional manner, etc.

From the above list, your staff knows that your messaging is "My manager is a stickler for punctuality, quality/timeliness of work product, and expects us to be professional when giving a presentation."

A final example of messaging could be your focus on the big picture of the company that includes:

- Meeting strategic organization goals

- Achieving quarterly results such as sales quotas

- Improving annual balance sheet figures, etc.

Hence, your staff knows your messaging is, "My manager is about the big picture of the company and meeting strategic goals," or "My manager is about meeting quarterly results, etc."

This legitimizes expectations and provides a theme that many managers are at a deficit with. How many times have your worked in a company where many divisions and division managers do not have a theme or expectations for their staff or have lost it over the years? Employees are usually less productive, and end up becoming lost in the organization. They are reflecting their manager's weak messaging or lack of messaging by their conduct and performance, and it is a direct reflection of him/her. That manager may be a talented employee, but when in the role of a manager, he/she needs to provide the direction and theme that puts their identity stamp on the work unit. This takes time but not as much as you may think when you set your messaging early on. People will get into a rhythm when it comes down to it. Once again, it all starts with leadership and flows downhill from there.

You have to be cautious that you do not have so many themes and expectations that your messaging confuses, frustrates, or wears out your staff. Keep in mind that many of the people who work for you are gifted with unlimited ideas and problem-solving abilities that you do not want to turn off by being overbearing. You do not want to appear to be imparting so many rules that you are labeled a control freak who has to have it your way or the highway.

It should be noted that your messaging might change over time, particularly as you mature as a manager and move from job to job and company to company. It is not unheard of to be proactive and modify your message depending upon what is needed at that point in time. The messaging that worked for you 10 years ago while managing at Company A may not be what you need now while managing at Company B. The same old message you have lived by may be less relevant today, excluding the integral and ethical ones of course. Therefore, you may need to adjust your messaging to better fit your staff and organization's style and realize a more effective result. This does not mean that you lose your identity as a manager because your messaging changes. It means that you are majoring on the major things and minoring on the minor things. Rearranging the deck chairs on the Titanic does not really help the overall situation in the end when change is what is needed!

External Messaging

So far, we have been talking about internal messaging. You also have to be aware of how those external to the work area you manage are receiving your messaging. An example of this was General George Patton, U.S. Army (1909-1945). He was considered by many to be a great leader but he did not adjust his messaging over time because his message was demonstratively defined by his curt personality. That type of messaging can sometimes turn into a conflict since it is personality driven. What was Patton's messaging? Arguably, "Be aggressive and take ground." That was his expectation of his staff and soldiers. His nickname became "Old Blood and Guts." However, with his success also came some dyer results to the men he led and the allies he interacted with. This cost him professionally. The result of his aggressive messaging during World War II produced battlefield results but took a toll on his men. It also transferred over to other areas that eventually rubbed his superiors the wrong way. The two separate incidents where he slapped enlisted men was the breaking point. He agitated General Eisenhower, Supreme Commander Allied Expeditionary Force in Europe, and some of the key ally figures to the point where it resulted in his removal as Commander of the U.S. Seventh Army. It almost sidelined him indefinitely for the duration of World War II, until he was reluctantly afforded a second and last chance of redemption. Because of his overbearing messaging and resulting actions, both internally and externally, he was relegated to being used as a decoy to distract the German military leading up to the allied D-Day invasion of Normandy, France, instead of being the point man to lead the invasion. The German military believed he would lead the allied invasion into France. His own superiors thought differently. Understand that this once successful and revered general was intentionally left out of the most important campaign of World

War II because his messaging did not adjust to where his organization was during that time of the war. Eisenhower had enough on his plate trying to get the allied military leadership (and their egos) to cooperate with one another without Patton sending another message inhibiting the organization's overall objectives.

As a talented manager, you do not want that to happen to you. We should be able to learn a key lesson from General Patton and not make the same mistakes. Simply adjusting your messaging is sometimes all that is needed to avoid being set back in your career. It is interesting how a person's style can impress one group of people and turn off another group. Similarly, you must always check your messaging to see if it is consistent with your organization's style and goals. Once again, it is good to be pioneering and bring a fresh perspective to your management position with your style — just make sure you do not try to reform the company by going overboard.

In today's day and age, you clearly see what often happens to sports coaches when they lose their messaging with their team. They end up "losing their team" or you may also have heard it said, "They lost their locker room." The overall result is that the wins start to drop off while internal dissatisfaction grows. They do not remain the coach long after that. Why? Because they lost their messaging, which caused them to lose their team, and the performance results clearly demonstrate that fact. Just as an organization can see positive results from a manager, they can also see negative ones. In the case of a struggling manager who has lost his/her messaging, higher-level management will eventually step in to make a decision if things do not turn around. They may choose to go another route by parting ways with the manager.

How to Get Your Messaging Back

What if you have been a manager for a while and come to the realization that you have lost your messaging? How do you get it back and re-establish yourself? Simply ask one of the following questions:

"What message do I want to relay to my staff at this point in my tenure with this company or organization?"

or

"What message do I want to relay to my staff at this point in my career?"

Understanding where your organization is during this phase of its business life and simultaneously where your career is will keep you from making the mistake of trying to be something (or have your staff become something) that your organization and its culture does not reflect. There is a fine line between being forward leaning and possessing a "tip of the spear" mentality, as a manager instead of becoming a wrong fit as a manager in an organization that does not support your style. Keep in mind only you can answer the question, "What message do I want to relay to my staff?" Remember, there is no wrong answer but only what you come to decide it should be. No one else has the internal perspective that you possess. You just have to apply the right approach at the right time, and you will achieve the right results that will set you apart as an effective manager. Consequently, this is what will eventually get you noticed. Why will it get you noticed? Because the results that your work area produces and the attitude your staff carries will be evident to all.

Overstaying a Position

On a final and overarching note, oftentimes managers and employees can remain in an organization or a position for so long that they ultimately lose their effectiveness. They are no longer a good fit with the company and where it is headed. *What they should have told you in undergraduate or graduate school is that we all have a shelf life on the position we currently occupy.* We all know of an employee who remained so long in their position that everyone in the workplace knew this person should have moved on years ago, whether it be to another job, another company, or retirement. Whether it is fair or not to make that kind of judgement on another colleague is dubious. However, it happens all the time and in any workplace where people know each other for an extended period and become familiar.

As a manager, you do not ever want to remain in a position so long that your messaging loses its efficacy. This can happen when you become too familiar with your tenured staff and vice versa. If you have new employees coming into your work area then this can be minimized. It is usually with your long-term staff that you have to be concerned when you see signs of this occurring. After an extended period of time, you may need to "freshen it up" and evaluate your current messaging to your staff and use that as a tool to bring a renewed sense of purpose to both the work area you manage and your career. Organizations change over time. Mission statements always seem to change, upper management changes, customers change, etc. You have to keep one eye on those elements while comparing it to your messaging and style. Bottom line, if you realize that you have lost your messaging and effectiveness as a manager, maybe you need to ask yourself the following questions: "Do I still belong here with this company or organization? If I still belong here, can I renew my messaging with my staff? Is it time for me to move on to somewhere else?" As I will share in Chapter 13, "Be Honest With Yourself and Grow."

CHAPTER 4

POLITICS OVER PRACTICAL

Many times, the politics inside an organization dominate the practical aspects of getting the job done. There is no master's level course for navigating through the world of office politics. Admittedly, some individuals are better at it than others. What you have to be aware of and understand upon entering a new company, organization, or division within your current workplace is: Who is in charge of what? What levels of authority do they have? How long they have been in their positions? Who are the decision makers? These elements are key as you navigate your work career in any organization. Once you have these questions answered you can artfully and successfully manage any project, program, or work division by strategically establishing your overall goals and laying in objectives, many times as they unfold over time. Simply put, it is like a game of chess that starts out with basic moves, and then it evolves in front of you causing you to identify and skillfully react in order to further your project, program, or division objectives.

In my career, I have tried operating under forthrightness and transparency, which is why many of my immediate supervisors and upper management liked me. Those traits can be uncommon in the business world when its dog-eat-dog, but they are quickly picked up by the people you will be working for. Years ago, I was told by a number of senior managers that it was refreshing for them to have someone with the courage to speak the truth when challenging situations would arise involving many competing factions. I remember one instance when I was a director in a large-sized organization and was invited to take part in a senior leadership meeting involving a new performance pay system that was going to be implemented. There were many skeptical voices who felt that the managers would simply reward their friends or favorites while overlooking the other employees. After I spoke directly to that point in the meeting, I could see the facial expressions of one or two of the senior leaders at the table who were blown away with my candid and transparent remarks. Being a straight shooter has its advantages in a politically charged environment or organization to influence outcomes. A strong tactic I employ is to be direct, face the situation early on in a meeting to diffuse it, as opposed to allowing the meeting to head in a direction that runs off course and gains momentum for untenable solutions.

You can come across as an impartial player in any multi-sided argument who provides truth and facts when skepticism and mistrust are dominating the atmosphere. This is where we get practical and dominate the political. You will find that too many people have wrong motivations in your organization and try to manipulate outcomes in their favor. It is understood that being politically savvy is important in today's age but being political does not have to be. What does one feel about another when they think of them as being political? In other words, they do not think they are being honest. Unfortunately, the words political and dishonesty have become synonymous.

Top Cover

So how does one operate and become politically savvy? One of the primary things you need is what is called "top cover" in the military. This means you should find those in authority at a higher level who can provide support and backing when you are unable to be in the room and your interests (you, your project/program, the work area you manage) are being discussed. This top cover comes from those who believe in you and your abilities within the organization. I talk more about this specifically in Chapter 11, "Men and Women Workforce Dynamics," under "Who's Your Sea Daddy?" section. *What they should have told you in undergraduate or graduate school is that you need someone in your organization to have your back when you become a manager.* Why? Because sooner or later you WILL tick someone off in management. This inevitably occurs when you are doing a good job and begin to be noticed for your steady achievements. From this, you will have a few jealous colleagues who feel threatened, try to derail your efforts, and inhibit your future success by doing undermining things, such as trying to limit your budgetary resourcing or reduce your project exposure. This is where your top cover comes into play — ensuring you are supported and protected.

Top Cover from Immediate Boss

You obtain this top cover by several means. First, through your immediate boss. Your primary goal as an employee, whether you are a manager or not, should be to make your boss' life easier, who will in turn provide you top cover in the form of support and protection. Be diligent not to cause him/her more work, but less. Make them look good by your contributions. Demonstrate that you are there to support them. This will get you the immediate first layer of top cover that you need. I have seen too many managers not do this and treat their immediate supervisor with indifference, especially with regard to them succeeding or failing in their respective position. Not good! How much support and effort would you provide a subordinate manager of yours who had this type of attitude and felt this way toward you as their boss? Would you want to provide them the top cover they needed when the occasion arose? When you get your boss' top cover, then you usually get their boss' top cover as well. Do you see how this works? I have personally benefited from this repeatedly. I recall one particular instance in which I was told after the fact that my boss really stuck up for me in a meeting with upper management when someone tried to undercut me and my work area. The undermining effort did not succeed because I had top cover.

Top Cover from Exposure

Second, you can obtain top cover by becoming more valuable in your company or organization by getting more exposure. This is accomplished by being on high profile projects or managing tougher assignments. When I was offered my first management position, others were also considered but they shied away from it for many reasons. They thought it was going to be a lot of work, require travel, possess personnel challenges, and have to deal with union issues. They were right in their assumptions. However, when I turned that work division around and achieved great success, the head of our organization took notice unbeknownst to me. As a result, when the organization restructured due to being acquired by a larger entity, he selected me to be one of his two direct reports as a regional director over the California and Nevada territory. He later told me that during a meeting to discuss this restructure, he stated to the group in the room that the type of person who was needed to lead one of these two brand new regional director positions was someone like me, John Balestrieri. His idea was strongly objected to by a senior manager who was selected to be the other regional director position. This manager did not care for me because of a previous confrontation we had with one another in which I privately called him out on an issue after his continual provocation. I was also two management layers subordinate to him at that time. (I was young then so you will have to pardon my youthful indiscretion.) In this case, the head of my organization provided me the top cover to elevate me to a very high position overnight.

Another method to gain exposure and obtain top cover is to volunteer for your company's favorite charity, and attend morale-building events or retirement ceremonies. Recognition from these will link your name to positive things. Why? The impression it leaves shows that you possess other intangible qualities that will be remembered once back at the office. It is amazing how you will be noticed and that in itself may be all you need to have your abilities highlighted and top cover to follow suit. It can work as easy as that!

Top Cover from Networking

Third, networking cannot be underestimated in gaining top cover. This will require some additional time inside and/or outside of your workday by taking part in extracurricular activities. However, you expand by networking outside the current work group that you manage. For example, I would volunteer to speak at the local chapter of a nationwide professional association during their bimonthly luncheons. They loved me as a result, not to mention that it honed my speaking skills and got me noticed by my colleagues in the regional area who were employed elsewhere. They were aware of my name, and I now had a voice when I would go to external meetings.

However, it could be something as simple as breaking away at lunchtime to go to the company gym, if they have one. I have met and personally gotten to know other managers and directors by simply interacting with them at the company gym. At first, we did not know each other or may have only seen one another at a meeting. After a while, a friendly work relationship developed from those workout interactions that served me well when I needed the top cover they were able to provide. This is because they got to know me and gauge my character better as we slipped some work-related issues into the exercise time, all of which occurred outside the normal office routine.

Your Organization's Culture

The next thing you need in order to operate and become politically savvy is to align yourself to the organization's culture. Do not fight it, or else leave it. Meaning, if they do things a certain way such as performance goals, manager expectations, dress code, communication styles, or whatever makes them have the culture they do, then get on board with it. If you are unable to do that due to personal beliefs or demonstrated unethical behavior that you encounter, then move to another organization. Do not get me wrong, it is perfectly acceptable to have your own slant on things and a sense of style as a manager.

However, you do not want to find yourself being halfway in and halfway out from a commitment perspective. Furthermore, simply existing in any work environment for a paycheck can be dreadful and depressing. Life is too short, and you are too talented.

One time I made the mistake of finding myself halfway in and halfway out commitment-wise after I was hired into a management position, and it cost me. I eventually became the odd man out, so to speak. I saw what was going on with management and their unethical methods. I could not believe these type of things were allowed to go on for so long. However, that is what happens when senior leadership allows bad behavior to persist and/or is a direct participant in it. At first, I thought I could make a difference to improve things but when I realized that I could not, I shut down internally and others could see it. I did not believe in the place any longer, and I certainly did not believe in their style of management. They in turn did not believe in me any longer. Looking back, I should have played it different, but life is our teacher, and I learned from those mistakes. I became more politically savvy (and successful) as I moved on to future positions.

CHAPTER 5

UNDERSTANDING LEADERSHIP

A leader is someone who people willingly follow, plain and simple. However, leadership is sometimes such an overused, misunderstood, and misapplied word. Are management and leadership synonymous? Is every manager a leader? Is every employee a leader? Is every parent a leader? And this line of questioning goes on and on. What do we get out of it when it is all said and done except confusion? I have been in training courses and read materials on the subject that pretty much stated everyone is a leader. Really? Only in America is it often considered second-rate to be a follower. For some reason, everyone needs to be the big chief and being a follower implies a lesser value. How untrue. Let's face it. We have all known many who were in positions of authority such as managers, project leads, teachers, coaches, celebrities, etc., who were not leaders. Why? Because it was not in them to be such as they were the wrong fit for the job. The position implicitly called for leadership skills that they did not possess, but somehow they got the job anyway. They were then thrust into a role that everyone automatically assumed they were prepared for to "show us the way." Could it be that innately, they did not possess the needed leadership traits, and no amount of training courses could produce those qualities?

When I was growing up, I had two parents who came out of what is considered the greatest generation. They had me later in their lives. My father was 50, and my mother 41 when I was born. My father earned five bronze stars as a Chief Petty Officer in the U.S. Navy during World War II. My mother was a teenager in Europe during the war and had to endure when the Nazis clamped down on the region of Tuscany where she lived. They both were fine people, unassuming (as many were from that era), and led their lives by example. As a boy, they taught me to be respectful, keep your hands to yourself, and get along with others. So that is what I did. They enrolled me in school a year earlier than I should have been so I was a year younger than the other students in my grade level. As a result, I automatically became a follower. I did not realize that I could become a leader until after college when I began my first job as an Industrial Engineer (IE). One of the reasons I chose this Engineering discipline was because it led the quickest to management. IE's had to take all the science and math courses as the other engineering students but were given additional courses in operations and business to prepare them more holistically. They were trained to be able to come into any business and improve operations, i.e. increase productivity, save money, improve processes, and just make things better. When I was in high school, we had a representative from the University of Pittsburgh visit our algebra class and explain the various type of engineering. When I heard her explain what an IE was and that Industrial Engineering was considered a business type of engineering, I said to myself, "That's it. That is what

I want to become." Consequently, I declared my major as an incoming freshman although it seemed like the rest of the world and fellow college undergraduates did not know what an IE was. Most students had heard about Electrical Engineering, Mechanical Engineering, and Civil Engineering. Additionally, many of the engineering students would say that IE meant "imaginary engineer" and the IE's response was that we would be their bosses one day. It was true that IE's were more likely to be managers over the other engineering disciplines in the workforce if they remained in engineering but most likely would become managers in other career fields.

Seven Basic Traits of a Good Leader

1. Vision

When I began my career as an engineer, I was part of a visionary recruiting effort created by the executive director to bring in around 15 or so IEs to be the future managers of the organization. Early on, they rotated us around to give us experience in different work centers. The plan was to place us in open management positions when vacancies would arise in any of those work centers. However, that did not happen for many of my fellow IE co-workers. I was fortunate enough to be selected to assume a very challenging role as my first management position. At 27 years old, I became the first civilian employee to be the production superintendent for the U.S. Navy's STANDARD missile and Tomahawk Missile Facilities in Seal Beach, CA, with approximately 70 personnel assigned to me. I was thrust into the role of a middle manager with the clear assignment to win the cost competition with our rival in another part of the country performing the same work. In other words, make the operations more cost effective or be put out of business and everyone loses their jobs. So, I became a division manager with four branch managers organizationally assigned under me. I had no prior work experience as a first level supervisor or post college training for this position but by the time of the job offer, I knew I was ready for the challenge. I had been working with this division for some time in a support role and knew I could make it better, all of it! And how could I make something better? Because I had the vision to do so. That is the first sign of good leadership, vision. A good leader has to have vision to see the potential in what he/she is given under their sphere of control.

2. Inspiration

Second, a leader has to be able to inspire those under them to rally behind their vision. People are looking to be part of something bigger than themselves and believe in something more important than themselves. My employees bought into me and not a mission statement. Why is that? Because mission statements change all the time, and my vision and inspiration were more tangible to them.

3. Personnel Placement

Next, a leader has the ability to place the right personnel into the right positions and hire the right types of people to fill vacancies. Leaders must have the ability to see giftedness in their workers and align them to the positions and in which they will excel. Many times we inherent the employees we are assigned to manage as a result of being hired into an established work area. My senior director once told me, "We will have true success when we turn over our entire staff," meaning the current inherited staff moves on and we bring in the personnel that fit our criteria. I thought about that for a while as to whether I agreed with it since it sounded a bit harsh. However, after a few years at the company, I realized he was correct. Success can still happen on the way, but it takes more effort to work with the incumbent staff you inherent and their established paradigms.

4. Taking Care of Staff

A leader takes care of his/her people. Show them that you care. This will buy you more in loyalty and extra effort with your employees than you can imagine and makes large deposits into the emotional bank account that you have with them.

5. Course-correction

Once a leader sets the vision, he/she has to be able to course-correct when needed. This is not so much about flexibility. It is about recognizing when something is amiss and then being open to receive input in order to make the proper adjustments to your vision's objectives, goals, and strategies if needed. Remember, it is your vision. You have to be driven and committed to it in order to stay the course and not be derailed by naysayers and circumstances. However, we have to face the fact that six to nine months from now, for example, may present different paths that need to be considered. This is simply because you and your organization have traveled some distance down a route as a result of you, the leader, being behind the wheel of the car and pressing the metaphorical accelerator.

6. Communication

Next, I want to add in communication. In this day and age, it is paramount to communicate in an effective manner. You have to be able to relay to your staff the "why" of doing things. The days of the boss telling his/her employees to just do it, and don't ask questions are over. People (employees) want to understand what is being exchanged for their efforts, especially the millennial generation. They do not want to be thought of as mindless robots. They need to feel a sense of empowerment, no matter how slight it may be, when performing their tasks. Do not underestimate this fact. Yes, it may be a little trying to have to explain more than you would like, but do not relate that to your authority being challenged. It is simply the era we live in. Use it for the positive by gaining trust with them. The more they understand your reasoning behind your decisions, the more they will grow with you and trust your future decisions with a little less questioning.

7. Trust

That leads me to the last and most important trait of good leadership, which is trust. I purposely left this for last to get your attention. You, as a leader, have to tie up the other six characteristics into a ball with trust as the twine. Trust is what holds everything together. If they trust you, they will follow you. If they do not trust you, they will not follow you. It is as simple as that. This trust factor holds true for the company as well. Meaning, if the employees trust the company, they will stay. If the employees do not trust the company or organization, they will ultimately leave. Believe it or not but your employees want to believe in you as a leader. It is a point of stability for them. They want to believe that you are the person they can place their faith in and who has answers to keep them pressing forward on their journey with the company. Without it, they feel less connected to the company and begin to look elsewhere for employment. No employee wants to come to work and feel in limbo because his or her leaders are untrustworthy and unreliable. Yes, trust and reliability go hand-in-hand. If the leader is trustworthy then he/she is also considered reliable. If the leader is untrustworthy, then he/she is also considered unreliable. It is all a matter of perception. Trust is perceived as well as acted out. Set an atmosphere of trust in your work environment. Employees can sense when you are trustworthy. Keeping your word and following through with your actions go a long way in leading by example. That sets the bar for them to emulate. You can be counted on as a rock of integrity whether you see yourself that way or not. Never make promises you cannot keep but, never fail to deliver on the ones you can make happen.

In recap, the seven basic traits of a good leader are:

1. **Vision**

2. **Inspiration**

3. **Personnel placement**

4. **Taking care of staff**

5. **Course-correction**

6. **Communication**

7. **Trust (the most important of all)**

Leadership for the Situation

There are books on leadership that tell us there are six, no seven, no 11, etc. different leadership styles. Some of those types are Autocratic, Democratic, Strategic, Transformational, Transactional, Servant, Laissez-faire, Situational, etc. You can certainly read one of those books to discover which type you may be more naturally aligned. Whichever style you identify with, you must remember that you will need to be able to adjust your leadership style to best match the business unit you are managing in order to have the greatest impact. This is what some may refer to as situational leadership.[1]

What they should have told you in undergraduate or graduate school is that one dimensional leadership types do not work as well today as they once did in years past. The main reason is technology. First, technology is evolving so rapidly that it is dramatically changing business models and processes that are much more complex to implement and support. Second, technology has also dramatically influenced the post-baby boomer generations of employees.

A modern leader has had to know how to handle the three primary generations in the workforce, which were baby boomer (1946-64), Generation X (Gen X) (1965-80), and millennial (1981-1996). Now, the Generation Z (Zoomer) (1997-2012) folks are entering the workforce with their own uniqueness that must be led. We are usually good with managing our generation and the one just prior to us because that was our parent's era, so we can relate. What we have trouble with the most is relating to and dealing with the employees in the generation or two after us. Basically, it can be said that baby boomers live to work and acquire things. Gen Xers desire a work-life balance. Millennials work to live, are less concerned about things (stuff), and desire actual experiences. I am an older Gen Xer. I can relate to baby boomers and my own Gen Xers well. We, Gen Xers, bridge the gap between those two generations. See Figure 1.

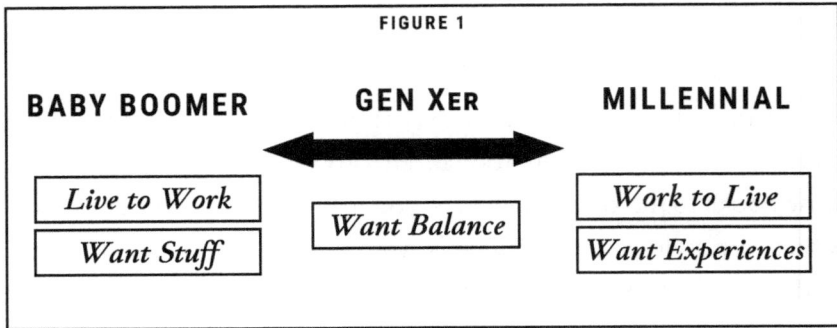

FIGURE 1

BABY BOOMER   **GEN XER**   **MILLENNIAL**

⬅━━━━━━━➡

Live to Work		*Work to Live*
Want Balance		
Want Stuff		*Want Experiences*

It seems like the focus today is on the baby boomer and millennial generations. You do not hear that much about Gen Xers. Baby boomers who are in charge in any organization are the ones writing policy for the workforce to follow that many times is out of touch with millennials, who are two generations away and make up a large faction that is supposed to comply. Does anyone see a problem brewing here, or is it just me? Consequently, who steps in to supply the sanity check to the boomers in charge while explaining to the millennials why this policy is important or even relevant? It is the Gen Xers. That's right, the generation of people who were into MTV, the Walkman, big hair for women, and the mullet for men.

Candidly speaking, it is a greater challenge to lead and manage millennials. In my experience, they are more delicate to handle and require more time, but they are very intelligent, extremely computer savvy, innovative, want to be empowered and feel ownership (do not underestimate that), need to understand the "why" behind things, do not want to be told they are wrong, and want to be kept informed. Therefore, to successfully lead any group of people you should adjust your leadership by utilizing the range of styles previously mentioned to match the environment in which you are working and the personnel working for you to maximize their ability and productivity. Keep in mind that you will have staff at different skill and ability levels not to mention fluctuating maturity levels. You will have variations of business processes and other complexities to consider. Therefore, you will need to adopt a specific leadership style based upon the reality you are in during that time frame. There will be a tendency to retreat to your natural leadership style, but as you read on you will understand why employing the proper leadership style for the situation is so valuable. Thus, you will be valuable to any company or organization because you have the ability to understand when and how to utilize a different leadership style based upon the situation.

During World War II, England chose Winston Churchill to lead them to victory over the Nazi regime. He had a way with words that could motivate the populace. In a famous speech to the English people at the beginning of World War II, Churchill attempted to lift their morale by giving them hope but wanted to relay how serious the situation was. He said, "I have nothing to offer but blood, toil, tears, and sweat."[2] That is what the English people bought into. However, in post-World War II the English people replaced Winston Churchill for a new prime minister. How could they choose to disregard all of the efforts that this great leader employed to unite the country and see them through the most difficult chapter in their country's history? One reason was his leadership style, which was perfect for that time of history requiring sacrifice and perseverance. In contrast, it was perceived to not translate well into a new era of recovery and growth that the country believed required something different from a leader. You see, not all leadership styles are ideal in any environment or organization. For example, you often hear companies or especially sports teams put out a statement when they replace a well-known leader with a new person that goes something like, "We are going in another direction." The new leader who was chosen will not be the same as the old leader or else they would not have replaced him/her. So what changed? Obviously, the leader did not adjust appropriately to their environment in order to be successful or show improvement, which is why they were replaced. You may have heard Bob Dylan's song, "The times, they are a changin'." Well, employees change, economic times change, organizations change, mission statements change, etc. As a leader, you have to be able to adjust your leadership style to maximize the talent and resources you have where you manage. This is more possible as years go by, and you become more mature due to extended work experiences under your belt.

If you start your own business, then you are automatically placed in a leadership role. If you are an entrepreneur who has successfully created and sold several businesses, then your leadership style could be the same throughout each venture. That is your model of success. However, there will eventually come a point when adjustments to your leadership style may be needed based upon the economic and business circumstances of the time and the sector you are in.

There are those who are natural leaders from the jump-start and it just flows out of them. It can be realized unconsciously at a young age especially if the individual is given an environment conducive to healthy emotional growth. However, most of us with leadership abilities will have to develop those inherent, dormant traits as we climb the ladder of success and look for management opportunities. Success and yes, failure, will be our teachers. Time will be our seasoning. The only way around this is to have a wise mentor. Someone who you can get advice from. This will help reduce your mistakes, increase your success rate, and decrease the time in the leadership learning curve process.

The ultimate culmination of your leadership style will be your ability to adjust to the work environment you are placed in. Accordingly, you will see a record of accomplishment that affords you a distinguishable and well-earned level of confidence when compared to your peers.

CHAPTER 6

WHAT ARE WE TRYING TO SOLVE HERE?

(Strategic Management vs.
Tactical Management)

Many times in management we get distracted in completing the "task at hand" and just getting the job done. We overlook the greater reason — like why we needed to accomplish that particular project or task in the first place. This is especially true if you are in an operations-type environment. We become so task-oriented that we default to what I call a Tactical Management approach as a management style. Do not misunderstand me, as there are many mundane and required duties we as managers must perform. However, it is not uncommon that when presented with a requirement, we pause for a moment to reflect back, and then ask, "Didn't we just handle this issue x number of months ago?" Well, the answer is yes, you probably did. The problem was that we were so pressed for time to complete that particular project/task that we did not solve it strategically, but only tactically. Meaning, we got the project/task done for now and moved onto something else not realizing it would reoccur later down the road and consume more of our time. There were times in my career that I could swear we kept reinventing the wheel on similar issues over and over again. Often, the reason for this was that our policy or internal controls were not in place, which would have allowed things to run smoothly. I used to tell my staff, if we encounter the same issue more than twice, I want a long-term solution documented and implemented across the department (or enterprise). We spend so much time chasing our tails on repeated issues because no one asked the bigger, long-term, and strategic question, "What are we trying to solve here?" How many times have you been in a meeting where you go down so many rabbit holes to the point where you ask yourself, "What is this meeting all about?" Then, once the meeting was over you ask, "Did we really accomplish anything?" That is what happens when managers and employees default to a Tactical Management approach when a Strategic Management approach was needed.

Strategic Management starts with the basic question, "What are we trying to solve here?" It then evolves to the second question, "Who are we going to impact?" The third question though is the whopper. It asks, "Why are we doing this?" or better yet, "What is the real requirement?" I find that the third question is not well received. Why is that? Because it challenges those who originated the project/task to provide full disclosure and be more vulnerable. The recipients of that question may feel it implies that they do not know what they are doing. That of course is not true, but perception becomes reality.

Furthermore, I find that the original intent of a project/task is not effectively communicated many times. The details of what needs to be done may be discussed and documented but even with a project scope, we march on like lemmings missing the mark.

Becoming an Industrial Engineer required me to study and learn project management. It was a mainstay for those of us who were attaining this type of degree. Our one operations professor had written over 20 books on the subject and drilled the main elements into us, which were Mission, Objectives, Goals and Strategies (MOGS). Some teachings simply interchange the G and O for MGOS. Thirty years later, it is still a part of my life. It seems to be more inherent for me to look beyond the short-term problem and go deeper, searching for a long-term solution to achieve optimal results. If you have a "problem-solving" type of personality with any hint of perfectionism, then you can attest to this as well. The bottom line is that it is effective to look at issues in the strategic manner versus tactical. Why? Because it all equates to time and money spent. Let's face the facts, our staff only has so much bandwidth that they can assume in their daily jobs.

I have discovered that large companies and organizations spend a lot of time and waste a lot of money on things that have never been challenged historically. These entities are similar to big machines that keep running while replacement parts (employees) are inserted repeatedly into them over time. The employees who come into a company jump into a system where the wheels have been turning for some time. They believe that the employees already working there and their predecessors have had the process running pretty well. Hence, they intrinsically believe and trust that the system has worked things out over time and simply follow the pre-established steps, not challenging the "Why?"

Being in management in the 21st century requires that you learn when to respectfully challenge the norm of direction from on high and when to "just do it" (meaning the project/task) while also completing the everyday duties you were hired to do. This separates you as a manager who just gets the job done to one who hits the mark. That is the difference between Tactical Management and Strategic Management. Much of what I am talking about is related to problem solving. *What they should have told you in undergraduate or graduate school is that problem solvers look for different ways to complete tasks and solve issues outside of the box and delve deeper than the tactical realm.* They move into the strategic realm without reinventing the wheel. When you go into the strategic realm, you have the ability to make things better, much better for the aggregate. Why? Because many do not connect the pieces at a higher level. In addition, most managers do not feel they can or have enough exposure to do so. Not true. Back to the three basics of Strategic Management:

1. **What are we trying to solve here?**

2. **Who are we going to impact?**

3. **Why are we doing this?** (Specifically, what is the real requirement?)

Let us break down each of the three Strategic Management questions.

1. What Are We Trying To Solve Here?

This has to be clearly identified and should be done in one sentence. Getting to the heart of the matter is essential so everyone in the room stays focused. You have to define the problem in order to correctly solve it. That means the whole story needs to be unveiled. Too many times I have been in meetings where half the story was presented when in reality, that was not the problem or issue. When we backed the truck up a few feet, we found the root cause and not just the symptoms. That is what you want to go for, the root cause. Do not let yourself or your team be distracted by symptoms of a process that is not working when it is the next, higher level you should be concerned with. That's what drove everyone to that particular process. For example when you are told, "We have to get another shipment out to customer Y," you can simply do that or you can go deeper. Was it just that customer Y wants more of that product or is our supply chain breaking down? Are we trying to fill in the gaps to meet that first order? Hence, if it is uncovered that customer Y is once again missing units from their latest shipment or the order was incorrect due to the continual ordering system glitches (or whatever else that leads to the root cause), then we have to be strategic and solve the real problem.

2. Who Are We Going To Impact?

You need to consider your sphere of influence. First, do you understand the problem well enough to know if it can be solved at your level, or does it need to go to another area or a higher level? Do you have the authority or responsibility in this area to solve the problem? When you provide a solution, will it be honored and implemented properly? Will the implemented solution cross over other work areas (divisions/ departments) requiring you to engage the proper stakeholders? Lastly, how is the customer going to be impacted by the problem we are attempting to solve? This is important because time impacts translate into money impacts. People impacts translate into money impacts.

Equipment impacts translate into money impacts. Do you see the pattern here? Thus, minimizing those effects on the customer is key. You want to aim for making the solution as painless as possible for the customer. That is how to maintain a good reputation and retain your clients.

3. Why Are We Doing This?

(Specifically, what is the real requirement?)

Is this really an issue and a necessity or simply nice to have? One way to ferret out the answer is to ask, "What is the real requirement that is driving this issue?" If it is a legitimate request or issue, then the reason provided should always clearly identify the problem you need to solve. Then you are able to understand the right amount of resources that are needed to provide an effective solution. If not, you will still be addressing the symptoms and not the root cause. People used to hate it when I asked, "What is the real requirement?" in a meeting. I could see the stunned look on the requesting managers' faces because it would destroy their whole premise for making whatever it was an issue when there was no real requirement. I was not trying to embarrass them. Simply, I was being strategic, and they were trying to stay tactical to get what they believed would solve their problem. So instead of answering the requirement question, they would sidestep it by providing some anecdotal response and never put any real teeth behind the request.

During these types of scenarios, I would look around the conference room table and see many people from different departments trying to solve something that was represented to be a legitimate problem to the organization. They were taking time out of their day believing they were being supportive and good team players by offering possible solutions and resources that their respective work area could provide. It was kind of like watching a group of folks at someone's house who decide to throw money into a pot to buy pizza. The only problem was that no one truly wanted pizza or was even hungry. A solution was offered and agreed upon that appeared acceptable to all. Bottom line, they had an answer to a problem that no one ever asked and produced a result that did not meet the true requirement. I am using the pizza analogy to drive home this point. They may have good intentions and even felt good about themselves after the fact for contributing to the pizza pot. Effort was made and some result was shown, which many believe is what matters. That is the tactical way of thinking and managing. Rise above that and be more effective by thinking in a strategic manner.

Do not just throw your resources into a pot believing you are solving a problem! Ask the tougher and more pointed questions like: "What are we trying to solve here?" "Who are we going to impact?" and "Why are we doing this?" Specifically, "What is the real requirement?" If you begin to think in this manner, you will be surprised how you can skillfully master the art of strategic problem solving and distinguish yourself as an effective manager who is able to think at the next higher management level.

CHAPTER 7

CHANGE MANAGEMENT

Greek philosopher Heraclitus said, "Change is the only constant in life." If that is true, then why is change so hard? Let's face it, we are all creatures of habit. When you get home after a long day's work, you probably have that favorite chair you sit in after dinner. You sleep on the same side of the bed. You always take two sugars with your coffee, etc. Nevertheless, we find ourselves in a work environment and wonder how it ended up that way. I used to tell my staff, "We inherit what people did or did not do before us arriving here."

Those with a change management disposition will not settle for status quo or allow things to remain in disarray. They simply want to make it better, whatever "it" is. A good change manager will always ask the hard question, "How did we get to this point?" regarding the respective issue in order to baseline the problem. Then, they will launch from there to solve it.

Change management can range from the organizational level

down to the project management level. The dictionary defines the term as the management of change and development within a business or similar organization.[1] To me, change management is merely taking an idea, system, or process and making it a working reality in your company or organization in order to improve its performance and effectiveness while overcoming challenges along the way. Examples include but are not limited to:

1. **Organizational change management to improve effectiveness via structure and internal alignment**

2. **System change management to improve technology**

3. **Process change management to improve performance**

Have you ever heard anyone in your workplace ask questions such as: Why do we have a branch office in one part of the country versus another, and what do they really do? Does the XYZ division in our company really make a difference to the bottom line? Why are we using this particular antiquated computer application to gather data and run these reports? Why do we spend so much money on travel? Why do we have the same ineffective staff meeting later in the week as we do earlier in the week, only called by another name that wastes another 1 ½ hours of our time? Why are there no career ladder positions in our department? How about business processes that you recognize should have been in place but are not, or are in place but they are outdated or ineffective? How about the selection process used to hire the staff you inherited before you became their manager? How about the inability to measure the productivity and overall effectiveness of a department when its staff's performance goals are not linked to the strategic goals of the company or organization? To further that last point, misaligned performance goals ultimately result in disorderly efforts and wastes resources since, when left to themselves, departments and work divisions will veer off and begin their own independent initiatives. Overall, these examples are areas that could be ripe for change management.

In my early years as an Industrial Engineer, I discovered that I had the natural ability to enter a workplace and quickly understand what worked well, what did not, and the gaps that existed. I would then make an analysis with recommendations and provide that to management in order to improve productivity. I would be able to do this while taking into account the various dynamics of the organization. This was a valuable skill set, as I became known as the "business process improvement guy." This was a precursor to my abilities in change management. My undergraduate training focused on the operational aspects of running companies and emphasized process improvement and re-engineering. This helped me immensely as I eventually became a very good change manager in my future management roles. I was hired many times into management positions not so much for my specific technical expertise of that particular job, but primarily because I could manage well, solve problems, and improve the overall running of the functional area I was in charge of. As I did this, I learned some valuable lessons and hard knocks along the way. What I have discovered in my extensive work experience is that it all boils down to three basic principles, which are: people, processes, and dollars. In other words, people performing processes which equates to dollars being executed. That of course, is an entirely new subject deserving of another book!

Reform

Companies are substituting a new word for change and that is reform. I guess it is believed that switching the name may cause the topic to be received better by the employees, sort of like "a spoonful of sugar makes the medicine go down."[2] If you ever watched the movie *O Brother, Where Art Thou?* there is a classic scene in the middle of the film where the Governor of Mississippi, Pappy O'Daniel, is sitting at a table in a restaurant talking with his brain trust about how his reelection prospects were looking for a second term in office. He is frustrated because his rival, Homer Stokes, has momentum and a slogan of "reform" (or change) that is swaying the electorate of the state. After Pappy's unhappy outburst at the table, his son says about Homer Stokes, "He's the reform candidate, daddy. People like that reform. Maybe we should get us some." Pappy in exasperation responds, "How we going to run reform when we're the incumbent?"[3] It is a funny scene, but oh so true. More or less Pappy is saying, we are the guys who have been entrenched here in this organization for some time and haven't felt the need to change. So frankly, why should we?

In the example, to admit the need for change is an admission by those in charge that things were not being run properly, and someone should be held responsible. That was not going to happen. Thus, ignorance is bliss. Everything is working OK, so to speak, until a real threat arises. This leads me to three of main reasons why change is so hard.

3 Reasons Change is Hard:

1. Organizational Design

But why is change so hard? First, the organizational design of your business dictates its ability to embrace change and then to actually make change. For example, in Chapter 1, "Organizational Design," we discussed the bureaucratic organization model. It is difficult to enact change within this type of an organization. Employees in any company or organization tend to become used to how it operates. Consequently, in the case of the widely used bureaucracy model, the system itself becomes so ingrained within the psyche of its employees that they will resist change. This resistance includes both strategic change throughout the organization and operational change within the department or work unit, all of which is meant to improve processes or policy if it is ever implemented.

2. Leaders Implement Change

The second reason change is so hard is because it usually takes leaders to implement change. *However, what they should have told you in undergraduate or graduate school is that leaders create change; managers sustain change.*[4] I am not saying that they both cannot be one in the same, but leaders are the visionaries who can see the future and communicate it as well. Managers are primarily operating in the now, problem solving and running the daily operations. Both are needed, but arguably one is more disposed to being the heartbeat of the company than the other when it comes to change.[4] Business schools in the past have primarily focused on educating students on specific areas of management and not so much on leadership. However, there seems to be an acknowledged movement in companies that recognize the need to develop leaders just as much as managers. I see this solidifying as we move into the future.

3. Political Capital

The third reason why change is so hard is due to the political capital that is required. I have found in my career that people in the workforce are usually relegated into one of three categories when it comes to change. One-third are open to it, ⅓ are closed to it, and the middle third are indifferent.

One of the key complaints I used to hear when a senior manager "came on board" (as they say in Navy lingo), was to enact some kind of change in order to demonstrate to their hierarchy they were being proactive, whether or not the change was needed. Everyone who worked for that manager, and even some peer managers, resented this approach since that person had only been on board for a short period of time. Do not be that person when you are new to a management level position! It is just like the standard response to the management interview question, "What would you do upon taking over this position if you were hired?" The proper response is, "I would observe for 60 days to understand the make-up of things (before I would consider any changes)." Well, you may have to wait a little longer than that unless there is some crisis requiring immediate attention. Initially, you have to build some political capital with your company/organization and some trust with your staff as well. This is important, especially if the change that you will be attempting to implement is sizable. You also do not want to be misled by the first one of your staff members who gets your ear on an issue, big or small. They may want you to enact some type of process change that is not beneficial to all parties involved. Sometimes these employees are biased, which results in a bad decision on your part. This can happen often to the new manager who falls prey to the crafty or disgruntled employee(s) who do not want to continue part of their current workload or may have an axe to grind with a rival division in the workplace.

Traditional Decision-Making Process

First, let us set the stage for traditional decision-making and then we will blend that into change management. It usually goes something like this:

1. Define the problem.

2. Clearly indicate what you want to achieve.

3. Gather and analyze the facts.

4. Develop a solution(s).

5. Make the decision to implement the solution(s).

6. Implement the solution(s).

7. Assess/measure the success of your solution(s).

That is how most people make a decision to solve a problem. This in a way, is a version of change, right? Simply speaking, it is moving from one position to another with the expectation for something to improve, and you probably do this subconsciously. That may be good for handling some situation outside of work where you are the sole stakeholder or main decision maker. However, there are other key factors to consider when change is involved. Those factors are presented next.

Change Management Key Factors:

1. **Vision**

2. **Buy-in from key stakeholders**

3. **Communication strategy**

4. **Traditional decision-making process steps (listed previously)**

5. **Sustaining the change**

1. Vision

Vision allows a person to see both the problem and the opportunity to advance things to another level, especially with regard to change management. Change managers can clearly see the reality of where things are at and then what it could look like in the future for the betterment. They will then inspire those around them regarding the change.

2. Buy-in From the Key Stakeholders

After receiving the illumination identifying the change needed, the change manager will look to obtain "buy-in" from the key stakeholders for the change initiative to have any chance of success. Initial agreement is not enough. I have seen directors and managers in a meeting nod their heads in agreement to a specific change proposal on one day, only to change their minds the next day because they did not fully buy-in to the initiative. You may know the solution that is required and what is exactly needed to implement the change. However, multiple stakeholders are usually involved in any company or organization whether they report to you or are located in other departments external to you. The greater and more expansive the change, the more buy-in you need from key stakeholders. You obtain buy-in by enacting a communication strategy that clearly establishes the need for the change.

3. Communication Strategy

A communication strategy falls into two parts. First, you have to present the impetus for the change, which should be out of urgency or strategic opportunity.[4] If it does not fall into either of those two categories then you will have a tough time achieving success. This is an important concept for you to grasp because people will always ask the same questions, which are: "Why are we doing this?" and "Didn't we try something like this a number of years ago?" You may fully understand the need for the change, but the other parties it affects may not. Therefore, getting them to understand and recognize the need for the change is paramount.

4. Traditional Decision-Making Process Steps

After you successfully gain stakeholder buy-in through an effective communications strategy, you can proceed with the traditional decision-making steps listed earlier in order to implement the change. Again, those were:

1. **Define the problem.**

2. **Clearly indicate what you want to achieve.**

3. **Gather and analyze the facts.**

4. **Develop a solution(s).**

5. **Make the decision to implement the solution(s).**

6. **Implement the solution(s).**

7. **Assess/measure the success of your solution(s).**

5. Sustain the Change

Once change is implemented, it must be sustainable. The new employees coming into your organization do not know any better, as they will think this is the way things have always been done. They are not the problem. The embedded culture of an organization is many times the real problem. It cannot be allowed to rise up and overthrow the implemented change once the change manager(s) moves on. Do not be fooled by the "wait them out" approach that often exists among the longer tenured employees, to include many managers. That passive resistance tactic may be lying dormant but can still emerge. It has been the number one technique used to undo transformation. To counter this approach, the change management team and/or leadership has to stick around long enough, past the first post-implementation cycle. This will help ingrain the new way of doing business into the culture and allow some of the kinks to be worked out. If not, the tenured employees simply wait out the change managers until they move on.

Another way to sustain change is to insert a measurable performance element into the appraisals of each manager or employee as necessary, and then grade them on their support of it. When an employee's evaluation has specific performance elements tied to their financial compensation, then the appropriate behavior follows suit.

Urgency and Strategic Opportunity

Urgency and strategic opportunity are the most effective ways to drive change.[4] I learned a hard lesson as a manager when I saw my efforts thwarted after a terrific organizational change management idea we had to centralize and standardize our entire travel program throughout the enterprise failed. The problem was that we did not convey the proper sense of urgency or strategic opportunity when we began this particular change initiative. It really was a great idea that had numerous financial advantages and other substantial benefits to the organization. The magnitude of this initiate was between $80 to $90 million being spent on travel each fiscal year. Our financial director was a leader who recognized the need to consolidate all the decentralized travel departments, which resided throughout our enterprise. This initiative would have solved several underlying problems and improved upon existing services, ultimately bettering the entire organization. Specifically, the plans included creating a West Coast office as the headquarters and providing greater hours of coverage to our travel customers in different time zones. In addition, we would be able to standardize the application of required financial entitlements to those same travel customers. This was not occurring due to subjective interpretations applied by our decentralized travel staffs in separate locations. Then we would be able to tackle the enterprise's volatile credit card delinquency rates incurred by its travelers. Furthermore, we could provide a career path for our employees in the travel field who felt like they were in dead-end jobs, improve their training, and reduce turnover for the travel staff. It would also allow the travel staff to perform officially required functions (such as in-depth audits and analysis that were required but were not being performed due to heavy workload). I could go on and on about the pluses to be realized from this change initiative.

So why was this change initiative not implemented? Did top management not support us? On the contrary, the top person in our organization was ready to back us. To provide some objectivity, I even brought in a UCLA MBA field project group to perform an independent study as part of their thesis project. This group was comprised of mid-career professionals with substantial corporate experience who were finishing their master's degrees at a top 15 ranked business school. They validated our proposed change initiative and had the data to show why this would be a big win for the organization. So what happened? Why did we not succeed with such a tremendous upside to invoke the change? The bottom line was that we failed to introduce the sense of urgency or strategic opportunity for the change we desired to effect. Then as time went by, the window of opportunity began to close for this particular change initiative. Those of us close to the change understood it perfectly, but we missed on the crucial communication strategy piece to get the buy-in we needed from key stakeholders below the top person in the organization. This was our failure. Those key stakeholders were the senior leaders who were in charge of each of the geographical locations of the organization. They were threatened by the potential loss of power and control that centralization and standardization would bring. From their perspective, they thought everything was OK with the status quo. They even cited how our enterprise tried this type of initiative years ago with our contracting department and "look at all the pain and frustration it caused," even though it was proven very successful two to three years after implementation. However, we never let these key stakeholders feel the pain of how out of compliance we were as an enterprise in our travel program such as: credit card delinquency rates, high volume of incorrect payments made, not to mention the frustrated employees in the travel divisions and their staff turnover. Bottom line, it was just a threat to them. We even offered the key stakeholders' three implementation options to choose from that would have allowed them to maintain control of their travel budgets and allow the same travel staff that currently worked for them to reside in their respective geographic area, but to no avail.

As the entire process dragged on, we did not recognize that our window of opportunity was beginning to close until it was too late. We were not as aggressive as we should have been with the implementation timeline, and we simply took too long. Consequently, unforeseen circumstances began to occur. The financial director, our champion, left our headquarters for another job and a new financial director was hired. My team and I tried to salvage the change initiative with one last effort. We wanted the new financial director to assume the mantel of champion. We explained to him our necessity to follow through on it since we were running out of time knowing that the top person (our top cover) in the company was going to be leaving in the not-too-distant future. He hesitantly and without passion tossed the concept out to the key stakeholders but could not get their buy-in. In fairness to him, how could he get buy-in without us having the essential communication strategy fully developed? In addition, he was new to the organization and did not possess the political capital in the enterprise, which is a key component for change to occur. When the top person in our organization eventually left, our window of opportunity closed.

If you look at the traditional decision-making steps listed earlier, the change needed was logical and well thought out operationally. It is not without saying that even technical brilliance cannot override basic human responses or political barriers. That leads me to the next point.

Emotional vs. Practical Component of Change

With respect to change in any workplace, I believe there is clearly an emotional component as well as a practical component. Pertaining to the emotional component, you have to take into account that there are those who have been working in a place for years and with that comes a certain sense of entitlement. You will be dealing with a paradigm that may go something like this: "I came to this company (or organization) and stayed here because I liked (fill in the blank) about this place, and I got used to the way they do things. But, most importantly, I bought in overall. Now you are saying it doesn't work (whatever it is) and by that, you are disrupting the stability and security I have put my trust in. I need to protect that paradigm and resist the proposed change because I still want to fit in here." Wow, if that premise is true, that is a lot to handle and dislodge from a person who now feels emotionally threatened. This is compounded by the anxiety and uncertainty they were feeling when the subject of change was first introduced to their work area.

Then, there is the practical component of the change. You are dealing with a paradigm by the employees that may go something like this: "What if the change doesn't work and they (whoever they in management are) get the change wrong? That's a lot of stress and burn-out that will be on us." As a manager, you have to consider this practical component and its potential ramifications which may include increased absenteeism, lower productivity, employee turnover, etc. But on the upside if "they" (whoever they in management are) get the change right, then its employees have the opportunity to become more creative, innovative, engaged, and develop an individual resilience which can translate to group resilience. This affects their extended sphere of influence within the workplace and can yield positive results, both tangible and intangible. Nevertheless, understanding both the emotional and practical components of change leads to ownership of the change.

Ownership

With regard to change management, many times employees view ownership as an "us vs. them" perspective. Thus, if "we" as managers mess up, then "they" as the rest of the staff told you so, i.e. that it would not work. In any workplace there has to be a level of trust by its employees. This allows it to overcome negative past experiences in which new initiative(s) that were attempted did not prove to be successful. This is why buy-in from the employees is also very important and not just with the key stakeholders at the upper management levels as discussed earlier. You need your staff to buy-in emotionally and have some skin in the game. Until then, it will remain an "us vs. them" mentality, which leaves management hanging out in the wind by themselves to take all the credit, or all of the blame, while trying to push this proverbial rock called "change" up the hill.

It is important to realize that employees who are high performers use change to their advantage. You can see it in their eyes and the way they carry themselves. As a manager, you need to identify those individuals and harness that certain "je ne sais quoi" they innately possess for both the success of the particular initiative and the good of the company or organization. Good employees like these spark other employees with their enthusiasm and sense of motivation, and that should not be underestimated. There can be junior leaders out on the office floor who make the difference between success and failure by carrying the consistent change message on behalf of the manager. The manager cannot always be the one overseeing the emotional make-up of their employees to ensure they are all rowing the boat in unison.

In Summary

The reward of solving significant problems within an organization and improving its performance through change management can be extremely exciting and beneficial to both the change manager and the company. However, buy-in from all the stakeholders is necessary for successful change to occur. Show the urgency for change or the strategic opportunity for change in a well-defined manner with a clear vision and how it will benefit all of the parties involved. If you can communicate in a convincing fashion, then you are 80% of the way home for a change management initiative to be successful. The actual work of change, where there is freedom to excel, is the remaining 20%, and that is the fun part of making it all come together.

CHAPTER 8

UNDERSTANDING AND HANDLING EMPLOYEE TURNOVER

All right, this is where the book is worth its money. Why do employees leave a company? That is the million dollar question, and if a company or organization could answer it correctly, then they could save enormous amounts of money. More importantly, and from a proactive standpoint, they could make a lot of money from employee retention that yields innovation and increased productivity by those who remain and the team(s) they work in. But aren't the real questions we need to ask, "What are the reasons an employee leaves a company, and what can be done early on to ensure they remain long term?"

Regardless of gender, the latest studies show that men and women leave their jobs at around the same rate and at every stage of a career from entry level to manager to senior manager, all the way up to the corporate suite executive positions.[1] In one sense, this levels the playing field by dispelling some of the better-known myths and assists in our reasoning process to get legitimate answers.

Turnover Rates

How much time, money, and productivity is lost to employee turnover? To answer that question you would have to calculate how long it takes, in months or years, for an employee to be fully integrated into the position they were hired to fill and become fully productive.

There are different percentages used to identify acceptable employee turnover rates. Some believe that a 7-8% per year is a norm to be expected for a healthy company. Others opine that if the turnover rate is kept between 10-12% per year, then it is acceptable. However, factor in the rule of 72 for whatever percentage you believe is the turnover rate for your work unit or company. That is the rate for a number to double; meaning divide your percentage number into 72 and that will tell you how many years it will take to "turnover" your entire staff. For example, a 12% per year turnover rate in your company divided by 72 equals six (72÷12= 6). This means that in six years, your entire staff will completely "turnover" or depart and new personnel will be in their place. (This is assuming the same people you hired in that same period do not leave).

Businesses with Longer Learning Curves

While employed with the Navy SEALs at their headquarters location in Coronado, CA, we had a higher than normal turnover rate. This situation posed a real dilemma that the upper leadership did not comprehend when it came to civilian employee staffing. For example, if we needed to hire an accountant, the technical expertise required was only one part of the position equation. Even if the person knew accounting well, the way that function was performed within the Naval Special Warfare organization was different compared to the rest of the Department of the Navy. The nuisances of the organization and in particular, how business was conducted, added to the length of time for that accountant to "come up to speed" and be fully productive. The range of time was usually between 1 ½ to 2 years. If this is similar in your workplace, then staffing and turnover takes on a more sobering tone. Consequently, when employees leave during a longer learning curve time frame while on their way to becoming fully functioning in their positions, it directly affects the development and sustainment of the rest of the staff. Specifically, this places more stress on the manager of that work unit and the remaining staff who now have to pick up the residual workload.

Starbucks Case Study

When I was in business school at the UCLA Anderson School of Management, we would use Harvard Business School case studies to review as part of the curriculum. Harvard Business case studies are used throughout a great many business schools as an ideal way to teach students that involves analyzing a real issue at a company and then attempting to apply solutions to a situation that has already occurred. The one case study that fascinated me the most was Starbucks. Historically, they have charged a premium for a cup of coffee and not simply for the experience they provide their customers or for profit's sake. Astutely, they fundamentally realized the immense cost of employee turnover to include the recruitment, training, and the period of time for an individual to become fully productive. To counter this dilemma, they provided the full and part-time employees healthcare benefits and a 401K in order to maintain a low turnover rate. And it worked! In this situation, the customer bears the burden of the cost to provide Starbucks employees these perks and obtain the added benefit of receiving their "skinny latte macchiato" just the way they like it! But is that it? Simply provide some extra "bennies" and the employees will stay? This case study caused me to dig deeper beyond employee benefits regarding turnover especially when I was confronted with it repeatedly as a hiring manager in various sized organizations. I began to delve deeper into the reasons employees leave for another position besides the familiar anecdotal ones.

Age and Pay

Let us start with the desire for more pay as the primary reason for employee turnover, to get that rationale out of the way. An employee can expect between a 5 and 10% salary increase as a result of changing jobs. That of course is dependent on the climate of the economy. A good economy would garner an employee the higher end percentage, which is between an 8 to 10% increase. However, I believe there is more to it.

Figure 1 is a symbol of the scales of justice to visually represent the balance of how age affects money as the prime motivation for taking a job. On the left hand side of the scale is age and on the right hand side of the scale is money. When employees are younger in their careers they will repeatedly leave their existing job for another one with money being a prime motivation. They will suffer through the rigors of the new job and if need be, muscle through the hardship of dealing with a difficult boss in fulfilling their desire to obtain a higher salary or financial compensation. (It is amazing what you will tolerate when you are younger when you look back on your career.) Accordingly, as Figure 2 demonstrates, the younger the age of an employee the more that money has a weight on their job decision making. However, as an employee advances up through the different stages of their career, age seems to have an equalizing effect in the motivation factor. This theory is displayed in Figure 3. As a person matures and acquires more positions throughout their career, their attitude begins to shift due to other factors. Marriage, children, geographic preferences, home affordability, etc. seem to factor in on future job decision making. As an employee gets older and progresses into their 40s, he/she has probably increased their salary to the point where they are becoming more comfortable and overall more settled. This is where another key motivation factor creeps up that many do not recognize, especially for employees at a larger company or organization. *What they should have told you in undergraduate or graduate school is that who you work for becomes more important than the money you make, as you get older.* You will know when that stage occurs with you personally, as it will be different for everyone. Make no mistake about it, a point in time will come when the "Is it worth it?" question becomes the mantra an employee lives by. The analogy I like to use is similar to having an apartment with roommates when you are younger, and you deal with both the good and bad. Then later in life, you buy your own place and enjoy the benefits of living without roommates. As many can attest, you do not necessarily want or need the ordeal of roommates any longer at that stage of life even though it can provide additional income. You simply like where you are in life. In the same instance, older employees do not want or need the headaches that go along with working for someone who makes their lives difficult only for a little more money in their paycheck. Figure 3 is a representation of this fact and shows that as an employee's age increases, their desire to have money as a prime motivation decreases.

FIGURE 1
Primary Job Motivations

FIGURE 2

FIGURE 3

Younger employees see money as prime motivation to leave for another position

Older employees see money as less of a prime motivation to leave for another position

JOHN BALESTRIERI

Why Do Employees Leave?

What are the some of the supposed reasons that employees leave a company or organization? The common answers are: higher pay, job dissatisfaction, promotion opportunities, better job title, improved working conditions, or better opportunities for advancement. However, let me give you the core reasons I believe why an employee leaves the majority of the time.

The Three-Legged Stool Theory

Figure 4 displays a three-legged stool and my proposed theorems for an employee to remain with or depart their place of employment. Each leg is equal in its function in supporting the person's overall job satisfaction level. One leg represents an employee's relationship with their boss. The second leg represents an employee's relationship with their co-workers. The third leg represents an employee's enjoyment or contentment in their job duties. As you observe the stool, note how two of the legs deal with relationships and the third leg is the actual job itself.

I believe the stool represents "connectedness" which is at the essence of a person needing to function as an employee within any workplace in today's environment. Furthermore, there is a new term emerging called "belonging," which is the same as connectedness. It translates as an employee needing a sense of community in the workplace, especially concerning millennials. It is more than likely that this need to belong, or feel connected, will continue on with Generation Z (those born after 1997) when they begin to populate the corporate workforce in the upcoming years.

Another one of the corroborating reasons I personally believe the three-legged stool theory rings true comes from another one of my mottos that I developed as a manager. It states that:

"At the end of your work career, you probably will not remember the projects you worked on so much as you will remember the quality of relationships you had at your workplaces and the bosses you worked for."

Then you will talk about if the job was interesting. These three attributes of boss, co-workers, and job duties are what drive many people to say, "Yeah, I liked working there," or "No, I did not like working there" when they talk about their previous employers. As you read further, I encourage you to test my theory with the people you know.

FIGURE 4

The Three-Legged Stool Theory

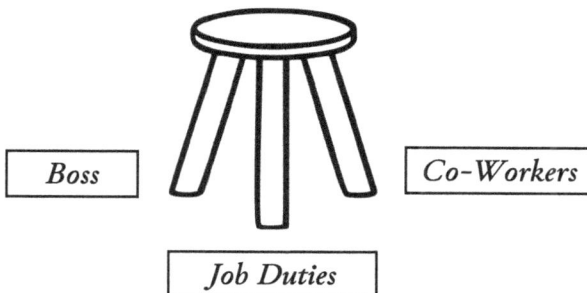

Boss

Co-Workers

Job Duties

Proposed Theorems:

1. Likelihood of an employee to remain with company/organization:

Like boss, like co-workers, not job = stay

Like boss, like job, not co-workers = stay

Like co-workers, like job, not boss = stay

2. Likelihood of an employee to depart company/organization:

Like boss, not co-workers, not job = go

Like job, not boss, not co-workers = go

Like co-workers, not job, not boss = go

Explaining the Three-Legged Stool Theory

For an employee to remain in their workplace, I believe they must have at least two out of the three legs in place. Three out of three legs is optimal. However, if a person does not have two out of the three legs in place then the likelihood of them departing their current position is high and more immediate.

In Theorem 1 for example, if a person likes their boss and their co-workers and has a good work relationship with them but does not necessarily like (but tolerates) what they do in their job, then they are less likely to depart. They will remain due to those relationships. If a person likes their boss and what they do in their job but not necessarily their co-workers, they are more likely to remain. If a person likes their co-workers and what they do in their job but not necessarily their boss, they are more likely stay put as well. However, if two out of three of those legs are not present, then the stool quickly falls. Theorem 2 represents this rationale. The employee cannot function well with only one leg of the stool in place. Figuratively and practically speaking it becomes too hard and almost impossible to maintain a healthy balance in that type of setting. The employee quickly comes to the realization that it is time for them to find a new stool, i.e. a new company or organization.

Every employee hopes to have all three legs firmly established at their workplace but frankly, that does not exist for most American employees. If you as an employee can attain two out of the three legs then you are doing pretty well and should strive for that third leg, even if you get to an "OK" instead of a full "like." However, if you currently possess all three legs as an employee at your place of employment then I applaud you and sincerely say, "Good for you!" On the converse, if you as the employer can monitor this balance and strive to ensure your employees maintain at least two out of the three legs, then you can reduce turnover and retain more of your workforce. The result you are looking for in the short term is to maintain or somewhat increase productivity. Then eventually you can look for big gains in the longer term due to the workforce stability you have created. This is the stage where hopefully innovation and trust can be present. When combined, these can empower the workforce to another level of performance.

Questions may always arise regarding this theory with respect to the link of money motivation and employee turnover. Specifically, "Do you mean that an employee won't leave for more money?" I did not say that. I discussed my one theory on pay earlier with regard to age. However, what I am attempting to show here is that if you as the employer can provide two or three of these legs, then the likelihood of the employee remaining with the company increases. If two out of three legs are gone, then there is no way that can happen. And yes, I have seen employees at all ages turn down moving to another company or organization for more money, better job title, better opportunities for advancement, or even improved working conditions because of having two of these three legs in place. Overall, you should not underestimate the power that the three-legged stool factors have on an employee's psyche and their desire to be part of a team and feel connected.

Buying Into You vs. Mission Statements

One thing that I would like to point out in employee retention is that there were many people that I have personally interviewed and hired who stayed with me longer than normally expected. Part of this was due to loyalty. However, the bigger reason they stayed was that they bought into me more so than the company or organization I was representing. During the interview process, they could see the enthusiasm I projected and my vision in building a team, and they wanted to be part of it. I was not simply touting my employer's brand name. You see, vision and mission statements can change quite frequently and so do product lines. People want to believe in something bigger than themselves and in someone they can follow. I was selling me, and they bought into that.

Holding Tightly To Employees

The one thing you have to be careful of is wanting to hold onto employees indefinitely. Similar to personal relationships, some employees are not meant to be with you long term. For example, they may be there to help in your transition phases or mid-growth phases at your company. I used to get upset when one of my employees left for another opportunity. Why was that? I believe it came down to expectations. I had an expectation and they had another, neither may have been expressed. So, when they left before I expected them to, especially after I put out time, money for training, and mentoring, I would take it a little personal and become disappointed with them. Certainly, communication between both parties about their professional development and career goals would help in managing these expectations. The bottom line is that you as a manager cannot take it personal when one of your employees departs. You may have a staff comprised of short term, mid-term, and long-term duration employees. This can be healthy and have pluses while you figure out the type of employees you believe will fit into your workplace on an enduring basis. Those employees are the ones you want to identify and put the extra time into. A caveat to this approach is that you must be careful not to place certain key positions in the short to mid-term duration categories, which can cripple your work area when they become vacant. This creates operational instability but can be avoided by you, the manager, by having an overarching viewpoint of your organizational staffing structure and how interdependent and independent positions should be within your company or work unit.

Building a Contender

For an organization's long-term success with the notion of wanting to be able to compete in the interim, I tend to look at it similar to a professional sports team that is building its roster in order to become a contender for the championship. That does not happen overnight. So how does a sports team fill its roster to be able to contend with its current competition yet have higher aspirations? Well, they have their current players on the roster, future draft picks coming out of college, and will recruit mid-level to seasoned veterans to fill needed gaps and who may be an upgrade to their team's current experience level.

From an employer's perspective, young people out of college may be talented with a lot of "upside" as they say, but are usually not too experienced. It takes time to bring them along and realize their abilities to be fully productive. In the interim, the team (company) looks to bring in free agents who are mid-level to seasoned veterans with the specialized skill sets that can help them win as many games as they can in the upcoming season. Many times these veterans (employees) can play into the long-term plans of the team and move from either the short-term or mid-term duration categories to the long term. That is what you would like to see occur when possible.

You have to win in cycles when it comes to staffing and dealing with turnover. It is a continual process that needs to be refined as employees exit and enter a company or organization. Always look to upgrade the current talent on your staff with individuals who are more dynamic than the person they are replacing and who possess a multifaceted skill set. If you employ this approach, do not be surprised when you look at your staff from where it was several years ago to now and not recognize many of the same faces you started with. That could merely mean that the team got better and kept upgrading its talent with personnel who fit into the long-term plans of the company or organization as it went through its phase(s) of growth and change. However, in any work area you manage, there has to be periods of staffing stability or else you will find yourself in a continual "do loop" always plugging gaps due to high rates of turnover. You, as the manager, will hopefully provide stability with your demeanor and experience by recognizing the growth phases your work area is going through.

As you become a mature manager, you should be able to understand employee turnover from a different paradigm compared to your earlier years in management. An astute sense should emerge to help you better understand if the turnover is systemic in nature requiring your attention or if it is merely the expected ebbs and flows of staffing that are a regular part of the business.

CHAPTER 9

HIRING/STAFFING

It could be said that hiring is a necessary evil for any manager. It is usually viewed as a compliance-type issue to be accomplished and then move on, similar to taking a bad tasting cold medicine. Yet, it is one of the most important aspects of being a successful manager since the outcome directly affects the manager and his/her work area. There are many in-depth books written on the subject that I would encourage you to read to increase your working level knowledge. In this chapter, I will attempt to streamline the process. The keys I would like to discuss will help you in the do's and don'ts in getting to the candidates you need to fill your vacant positions.

Many times when a position becomes vacant, the immediate supervisor unconsciously notifies Human Resources (HR) to let them know of his/her need to fill it. HR complies and provides them next steps and away they all go, down the hiring path. Unfortunately, that is not the correct sequence of events that should be transpiring. However, this is the "ready, fire, aim" approach that we all robotically go through when we react to a situation from an operational perspective. *What they should have told you in undergraduate or graduate school is that when a manager is sloppy on the back end of the staffing process, it will ultimately affect them on the front end when they have to deal with managing the work and respective workload of their employees.* I will endeavor to discuss the three aspects of the "back end" (preparation) of the staffing process.

1. Validate the Position

The first thing that should occur upon realizing a position will be vacated is to validate the position to ensure all of its duties and its alignment within the department are current. As the pace of business increases, I have found the attitude among managers toward addressing their subordinate staff positions and specifically the associated duties, has not. Frankly, it can be a burden and somewhat painstaking to review a position description, if one even exists, to see if it is current. Many are not. The following issues are usually evident in current position descriptions:

- The listed duties assigned to the position have changed

- The technology required and utilized for proficiency in the job has become outdated

- The position refers to a reporting relationship(s) that no longer exists

There is nothing worse to an employee when their duties are not clearly defined, too many grey areas exist, and unforeseen collateral duties inundate their daily job. Even if they are written on a paper napkin, you need to list the major duties of what you expect from each position that resides within your work unit.

A Full-Time Equivalent (FTE) employee equates to about 2,088 work hours in a year. Vacation, holidays, and personal/sick days can reduce the productive hours to 1,800 per year, depending on the seniority of the person. Productive hours refer to the time, in hours, that you can expect your employees to be on the job. Let us assume the position will conservatively receive two weeks of vacation, six national holidays, and four days of personal/sick days in a year. This amounts to 160 hours. That means your productive hours are now 1,928 at the upper range. For the more tenured employees, the productive hours may be more around 1,800 at the lower range. Regardless of the math you use, both of those numbers result in a large amount of work hours that can have a positive and potent effect on a work unit, if focused in the right areas. That is why it is so important to ensure that the position is aligned to the mission (purpose) of the company or organization. It should also be aligned to the function of the department that it resides in. There have been many times where I have uncovered aged positions within the company that no longer aligned to where it was heading. The once valid initiative(s) these positions were created to support became obsolete years ago. To make matters worse, management never reviewed or updated the position for potential realignment.

Do the duties of the job fit with the current direction of the company or organization and the latest expectation of the department it resides in? These are the requirements that need validation even if it is an indirect or support position, (i.e., finance, HR, safety, etc.) that enables the direct labor portion of the company. What usually occurs in these cases is that the requirements of the position changed over time, but the person encumbering it did not and so their acquired skill set and abilities became obsolete. Then, management did not take the time to reassess the position and realign it for optimal use. They also may not have wanted to have the uncomfortable confrontation with the employee about realigning his/her job let alone developing a plan to retrain them or worst-case scenario, lay them off work. No one wants to be told by their manager that their position is no longer needed. Transferring an employee can be an option. However, I have found that when it comes to transferring an employee to another work unit, the other managers in the organization view it with the same skepticism of "beware of Greeks bearing gifts." No offense meant if you are Greek! They will probably not want to take this displaced employee off someone's hands unless directed from higher management. Additionally, the incumbent manager may not want to lose the FTE that has to transfer with the employee if mandated. So unfortunately, status quo remains.

2. Determine the Reporting Relationship of the Position

Second, you need to clearly determine what reporting relationship you want the incumbent of that position to have with their immediate supervisor and co-workers. Regardless of the size of the company, the employee needs to know who they report to, take direction from, and will be supported by. These small internal alignments I am mentioning here roll up into the greater overall alignment within the organization. You may not necessarily be in, or desire the bureaucratic organizational model discussed in Chapter 1, which is fine. However, the employee needs some kind of reporting structure in order to feel grounded so they do not believe they are out there on the edge by themselves. Furthermore, the reporting relationship also identifies how independent you expect the position to function given the supervisory controls they are placed under. The less senior the position, the less independent you expect the employee to be. The more senior the position, the more independent you expect the employee to be. Thus, the work product will be evidence of that independence. All of this drives the position's salary and grade level.

3. Determine the Salary Range & Grade Level of the Position

Third, based on the first two criteria mentioned previously, you are now able to determine the salary range and grade level of the position. Many companies have predetermined salary ranges for their positions that HR maintains and were approved by the finance department. Payroll is usually the largest cost of any organization so the finance people have a say with regard to current and new position salaries.

Employees do talk and compare, especially their salaries and bonuses. They desire fairness, perceived or real, for the work they perform on the job. Employees become very disgruntled when they discover the person sitting next to them is making more money than they are while performing the same types of duties and have similar levels of responsibilities. These disparities can result in an adverse relationship with their manager. Overall, you want to avoid these problems as much as possible by ensuring the salary range and grade levels in your work unit are representative of the position's duties and its level of responsibilities.

Overhire and Shelf Life

You must be aware of the caliber of the individual you hire into any respective job. Hiring for a position cannot be thought of as a one shot occurrence without any growth potential unless that is the type of individual you want to perform that particular kind of job. If you hire high performers then you will have to show them some kind of a career path within your organization. They look for these things. To "overhire" a person into a position can make the individual feel unchallenged after a while, and they become restless wanting to move on. By the term "overhire" I mean the person possesses more abilities than the job requires, thus creating a job mismatch. As mentioned in Chapter 3, "Don't Lose Your Messaging," every person has what I call a "shelf life" in the position he/she encumbers. The shelf life could be two years, four years, seven years, etc. However, when an employee is too talented for the position and has no upward mobility, their shelf life becomes increasingly shortened.

Job Fit: The Right Fit Approach

Job fit is something I employ in all of my hiring selections. I personally call it "the right fit approach." It is selecting the best person for that particular position who possesses the right personality to go along with the other characteristics we were looking for in a candidate to complement our team and where we are heading in the future. It is not necessarily the most intelligent or hardest worker that I select to fill a position. When employed properly, the right fit approach can help address known weaknesses in your workforce.

The Right Fit Through Interview Questions

Since staffing takes time and effort, you do not want to repeat the process on a frequent basis because of high turnover rates. Therefore, during the interview process, you will need to employ a method to identify the right fit for the position you want to fill from among the many candidates. This can be accomplished through the types of interview questions you employ.

Interview questions fall into two categories, hard skills and soft skills. The hard skill questions are those that look to reveal the technical abilities of the individual that are relevant to that job. They should convey the aptitude and intelligence of the person. The soft skill questions are what drives the person's make up and truly reveals who they are. I like to ask candidates these types of questions focusing on how they respond.

I tell all of the candidates two things in the beginning of the interview. First, that there are no right or wrong answers to the interview questions. Second, we are trying to assess the right fit for our organization. The interview should be a win-win for both parties and not just one-sided because both parties have a stake in this impending professional relationship. I am not trying to play "stump the chump" with my questions as I have seen many managers do when conducting interviews. I want to observe and listen to how they process the answers to the questions. This will also bring out their personality and fit.

Interview Questions:

1. I begin each interview by asking, *"Can you give me a brief synopsis of what you do in your current position?"* Now, I have their résumé in front of me and have reviewed it. The résumé got them the interview. Their interview and the success thereof, is what gets them the job. From the question above, I want to see how concise they can be in formulating a clear and succinct response to something they do and know. Their response will tell you how well they will be able to provide

you a clear and succinct answer to situations or problems when working for you in the future.

2. Then I move to the hard skill (or technical) questions such as: *"Describe your knowledge of_____?,"* and *"Describe your experience in_____?,"* etc. Be specific especially if you are looking to address a particular technical weakness that you want to rectify within your work unit.

3. Then I switch to the soft skill questions. *"Tell me about a time in your current position when you were presented with an XYZ type of dilemma, and how did you handle it?"* As the interviewer, you can fill in the blank for the "XYZ type of dilemma" with something like a short fused assignment/task, a demanding customer, an uncooperative but important stakeholder essential for overall project success, etc. Observe their ability to respond and the logic process they employed to resolve that particular situation. Also, watch where their eyes go when they respond to the question. If they turn up to the left, it may mean they are recalling actual information from their past experiences. If they turn up to the right, it may mean they are creating new information, i.e. fabricating something.

4. *"Tell me about your worst professional failure, and how did you recovered from it?"* Here, I am looking to see how self-aware they are. Believe it or not but the answer I have received to that question a few times is, "I have never failed." Really? I was thinking to myself, "You have never failed?" Wow! The lack of self-awareness will always prove to be a problem when managing this type of employee. Candidates who respond in this manner either have a lot of pride or do not understand themselves much at all. In either case, it says a lot about them. This is not a good thing unless they are very young and do not have much work experience. If youth is the case, then maybe you can

have them link the question to a college or high school course or some type of summer job. Frankly speaking, we have all failed in some way or another professionally. This is especially true of those who desire to grow and stretch themselves or who are risk-takers. Mature responses to this question will identify their ability to accept responsibility and reveal what type of person they are. To admit failure is hard enough. However, to acknowledge the fact that it occurred, relay what they learned from it, and how they improved as a person, shows character.

5. *"What would your previous supervisors say about you?"* This provides another insight into the candidate by attempting to have them look at themselves from another person's perspective besides their own. Many have hesitated and then responded with, "Well, I can tell you what my previous supervisors have actually said to me," which is great.

6. *"Tell me your three greatest strengths that you will bring to this position."* These responses are good to hear, as I will then compare their answer to the other candidates that I interview for this same position. Yes, it is true that many interviewees have their responses rehearsed with regard to the three strengths and weaknesses questions. However, keep in mind the strengths they list should match up with the other parts of their interview and show consistency. It really is telling!

7. At the end of the interview, I always like to ask, *"Why do you want to work here for XYZ Company?"* This provides them an opportunity to show how much due diligence they have done in researching your company or organization. You will see their enthusiasm usually rise at this point with an associated facial expression to accompany it if they are indeed excited about joining your team. It can also provide a glimpse into how long they plan to stay with your organization. For example, there were occasions when an employee announced he/she

was leaving our company that I could reflect back to the interview I had with them and their response to this question. Specifically, their short-lived stay at our company and impending departure matched their response to that question when I actually recalled it. One thing to note in asking this question is that either directly or indirectly it should reveal if the candidate is simply looking for a job, or for more money than they are making in their current position. You do not want those reasons as primary motivators for a potential employee as they will not remain with you long.

8. Once you have concluded your interviews always follow through with the top candidate's references before making the selection. I prefer to contact the immediate supervisor of each of their two previously held jobs prior to their current one. I believe it is proper to do so because those managers will be more at liberty to convey their true feelings about the candidate and his/her performance ability.

These types of interview questions should be able to provide you a better feel for who the candidates are and identity the fit they would have within your workplace if hired. I have interviewed some talented individuals who I had to pass on but who many managers would have selected to hire. They were competent, but I knew they would not fit well within the organization, my work unit, or the team I was trying to build. The times that I have gone against this judgement has proven to be a mistake that ultimately resulted in another work gap that I had to refill, as the employee departed for another job shortly thereafter. I would have to start the staffing process all over again. Then, once the position is eventually filled, there is the inherent training curve both in technical ability and in understanding the organization/work unit and how it operates, which is never a short period.

Remember, you do not just want a technically competent person but one who will be the right fit for the position, work unit, team, and organization. Also, make staffing decisions that address known weaknesses in your workforce. Sometimes managers just choose the "better" qualified candidate from those who are available to them and not necessarily the "best" qualified candidate. Simply choosing the "tallest pigmy," as I heard my HR professor once refer to it, is not the answer. Meaning, choosing the best candidate from what you have in front of you knowing they are still lacking in abilities or skill sets is not a long-term solution. You may "stop gap" the problem for a while but eventually run into the dilemma of what to do with an employee who will not be able to meet the requirements of the job for which you hired them. This creates other sorts of problems with consequences. If you have to interview a few more candidates to get to the right candidate, then use your gut instinct and do so.

One final note, avoid internal nepotism when trying to fill more senior or lead positions, especially when the experience and leadership potential do not necessarily reside within your work unit. Many managers feel compelled to select one of their current staff members out of a sense of obligation to them. At that time, you must bring in people from the outside to fill these positions until you can create a pipeline that allows you to promote from within. The "grow your own" concept is an effective model to use, but until then you have to bring in free agents to help you get to that point.

Henceforward, when selecting a person with regard to the right fit in filling your vacant position, follow the wise counsel of the Grail Knight in the one movie scene of *Indiana Jones and the Last Crusade*. If you recall from the movie, Indiana finally makes his way into the cave where the Holy Grail is located. His foe follows him in and asks the Grail Knight which cup he should choose, as there were so many which seemed to be acceptable. The Grail Knight stated simply and profoundly, "Choose wisely."[1] I believe you get my analogy as I echo the Grail Knight's sentiment. When it comes to hiring, "Choose wisely!"

CHAPTER 10

DEVELOPING YOUR EMPLOYEES

Job Assignments

A crucial and often overlooked aspect in retaining an employee on staff and increasing their value to the organization is employee development. I would like to focus on what I believe is the major element of this aspect, which is job assignments. Employees need to be stretched from time to time so they do not fall into a rut. This is true regardless of how transactional or mundane their job is. They have to feel uncomfortable once in a while for their own professional well-being. Once again, the human default is to avoid any discomfort. I understand that. However, there is nothing worse for any employee than to be in an unchallenging job with no sparks flying around every now and then. Now, I am not talking about work drama. I do not care for that at all. What we as managers need to do is be able to identify the giftedness and potential in an employee and believe in them enough to stretch them with a tough assignment that gets their juices going and brings out the best (or worst) in them. Yes, there may be some complaining and grumbling by him/her. However, when they understand the importance of the assignment to you as the manager and how you believe in them to accomplish it, then they will put both legs into the water and not just one big toe.

Your Style

When you come into a company or organization as a manager or internally transfer to a new division, you will most likely inherent a staff of employees that are unfamiliar with you and your style. Likewise, you will be unfamiliar with them and their abilities. The question becomes, "How do you begin to meet your work responsibilities as a manager for the area you are in charge of while your employees adapt to you and vice versa?"

Many times the exercise of management can be clearly defined in distinct movements while at other times it is by spirit and intent. Both can be effective. However, here you want to be deliberate and set the stage when you first assume that particular management role in your first 180 days. *What they should have told you in undergraduate or graduate school is that the first 180 days is where you have to work the hardest as a manager — trying to prove yourself to both your new boss who selected you and your employees who did not.* There seems to be an underlying pressure to demonstrate to all parties that the selecting official (to include the organization's management overall) did not make a mistake in placing you in that position. Your employees will observe you in order to find out what you are really like. Make no mistake about that. The positive aspect is that it becomes your chance to sculpt them, whether a little or a lot, depending on what they demonstrate to you in the professional arena.

I have developed what I call the Four Stages of Employee Development. I believe it is an excellent tool that a manager can successfully employ in the development of an employee to become a high performer. As shown in Figure 1, you begin to take an employee through the four stages of employee development with the ultimate goal of achieving the last two stages with them. If you can do that, you can have a highly productive work unit. Notice that I did not say, "Have them achieve the last two stages by themselves." But it is achieving the last two stages with them.

As you move through the stages together, your interactions eventually become a rhythm between you and the employee that are attained together similar to a wave in the ocean that ebbs and flows as it heads toward shore. That may sound philosophical, but once you get on the same page with one another, as manager to employee and employee to manager, then you will appreciate what I am saying. Simply put, you will better understand how each other functions. At first, this may not be the case at all. However, you as the manager lead in this dance and your partner (employee) will follow suit.

Four Stages of Employee Development

FIGURE 1

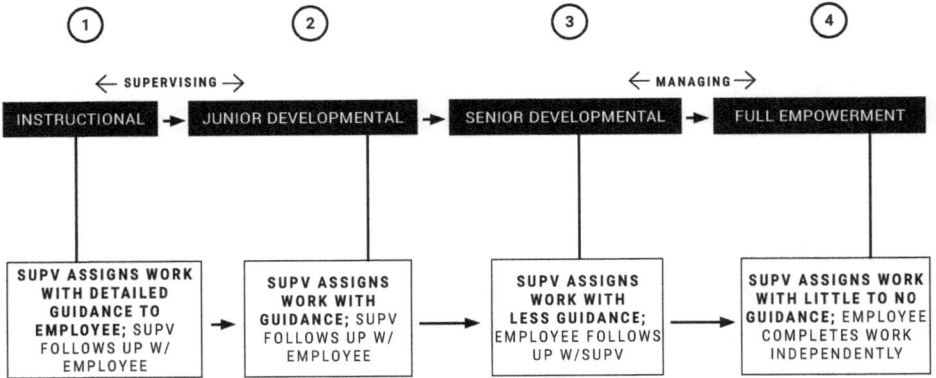

1. Instructional

The first stage is the "Instructional" stage in employee development. What this phase means is that you as the immediate supervisor assign work to the employee(s) with detailed guidance and explain the work product you want to see achieved and how you want it presented. During this stage, you will repeatedly check on their progress via scheduled meetings and "drive-by's" at their desk to see if they are achieving the key points that you laid out in your tasking of them in order to keep the project/task on track for completion. For example, if you are a new manager in a work unit and presented with a project/task to be completed for upper management, you would be more exact in laying out the requirements to your staff to accomplish it. At this stage, you may not yet know their abilities or have a format to use for a project/task similar to this one. The employee(s) could also be new or newer in their position(s) and lack experience. All you know is that you need to provide a quality product to upper management and hopefully meet and/or exceed their expectation in doing so. From this pseudo on-the-job training scenario, you get the opportunity to complete a needed task while beginning to sculpt your employees in the process. You want to provide them enough detailed guidance to understand your style and expectations while not overly micromanaging and thus inferring you do not believe they are competent. Never do that! Your employees want to know that you believe in them. This is where communication comes into play. You explain things more in this stage at first, which is done in order for you and them to understand each other's styles and your expectations as a manager. It can be as transparent as you want it to be.

Depending on the newness and experience level of your staff and the type of work unit it is, you should not remain in the Instructional stage for a long period of time. Sometimes the time frame is lessoned and even eliminated with certain employees due to their experience, learning ability, and maturity level. That acceleration can be beneficial for everyone so you are not dotting i's and crossing t's, relegating your employees to believe they are working for a compulsive manager.

This instructional technique will not be used for every work assignment but once again, it is used enough that the employee(s) pick up your style and expectations and you get to understand their abilities. Trust will then start to build after a few iterations of these "sculpting" or on-the-job training sessions, which is when you need to quickly move from the Instructional stage to the next stage which is Junior Developmental.

2. Junior Developmental

The next stage is the Junior Developmental stage. What this phase means is that you, as the immediate supervisor, assign work to your employee(s) with guidance, continually follow-up on their progress, and routinely correct their errors to improve upon their work product until completion. You want to be the initiator of the follow-up discussions with the employee but more like a coach who desires his players execute the game plan that he/she designed. Similar to the Instructional stage you will check on their progress via scheduled meetings and "drive-by's" at their desk to see how things are progressing to keep the project/task on track for completion. However, you will do this less frequently than in the Instructional stage so as to provide them more room to grow under your management style. You should provide them an environment to ask questions and identify any roadblocks they foresee to achieve completion. Just like in football, the coach calls the plays, makes adjustments when necessary with his personnel, and takes player input to help them improve on the next offensive possession.

This stage is especially important when developing junior employees, hence the name Junior Developmental. They will need this type of involvement by you, their manager, while they gain confidence in themselves and their peers. There is a "time to reward" relationship that pays off for the company when an employee eventually turns the corner and begins to gain effective results in their work assignments. From the broader perspective, the early stages of employee development has the company putting more into the individual than it receives until this occurs. Thus, the company may not always get the full benefit from the salary it pays out early on during the employee's learning and developmental curve.

It is good to remember that coaches do not execute plays, players do. Therefore in the same vein, managers do not complete the work assignments, employees do. You would prefer them to make mistakes at this stage so together you can work through them instead of having fundamental errors occur at the subsequent stages. More importantly, you want their proverbial house to be built on a strong foundation. The groundwork is laid at the Junior Developmental stage to evaluate an employee in order to launch them to the next level. Unfortunately, many employees find themselves stuck in this stage and never progress to the next performance level. However, that is not conducive to a highly functioning work unit. You want to see growth in your employees at this phase to be able to move them onto the Senior Developmental stage.

3. Senior Developmental

The next stage is the Senior Developmental stage. What this phase means is that you as the immediate supervisor assign work to your employee(s) with less guidance but now the employee(s) follow up with you until completion. In this stage, the guidance you provide is more of a general outline type of format for them to work with, either verbal or in writing. The employee(s) will be the initiator of the follow-up discussions with you, their supervisor, gaining your input on critical decision points and advice on larger obstacles. They will let you know what support they need. Counter to the Junior Developmental stage, the employee(s) is required to check in with you and provide their progress via scheduled meetings and/or "drive-by's" at your desk to let you know how things are progressing to keep the project/task on track for completion.

If we stay with the football analogy, the employee is now similar to the veteran quarterback who is executing the game plan prepared by you, the coach. However, the veteran quarterback is authorized more latitude to make decisions on the field and adjust to the different scenarios that present themselves without constant reliance on the coach to instruct him/her on what exactly to do. The quarterback is now acting more like the coach on the field and is empowered to call more of the plays. He/she just needs your support and backing. This is where you as the supervisor transition into a manager role. You will now "manage" the employee(s) and their work product by empowering them more in order to excel. Specifically, you will provide them support along the way until the completion of their assignment(s). You still set the expectations of the work assignment and the respective due dates. However, you allow the employee to grow by having him/her own more of the process through empowerment. That is the buy-in you want from every employee. Once they begin to attain ownership of assignments and feel empowered, they will inherently utilize their abilities and skill sets to achieve a quality product. If this is where you as the supervisor transition into a manager role, then this is the point where they, as an employee, transition into the role of becoming a higher-level producer.

For any company or organization to become high performing it must have its employees operate in the third and fourth stages which are Senior Developmental and Full Empowerment. Otherwise, it is no more than a transaction-based organization like the Department of Motor Vehicles (DMV). There, the supervisors are the ones who hold things together and consequently, carry the strain and burden of this type of organization. However, if it is a transaction-based type of business you are in, then that may be perfectly acceptable and all you need. For example, if it simply having the customer step up to the counter and order an item off the menu at a fast food restaurant, your expectation is for the employee to take the order, collect the money, and deliver the food to the tray. The post office is another transaction-based organization. The employee behind the counter takes the package, weighs it, assigns postage due, and collects the money from the customer. You probably do not want them deviating too much from that. However, if the goal is to become a high performing organization, then managers need to get employees functioning in the last two stages.

4. Full Empowerment

The final stage is the Full Empowerment stage. We, as managers, would LOVE to have all of our employees operating in this stage. What this phase means is that you as the immediate supervisor assign work to your employee(s) with little or no guidance and the employee(s) delivers a final product with minimal oversight or input from you. Here, the employee(s) is functioning at a very high level, can be trusted to make the proper adjustments, and knows how to work through complicated issues. They are able to overcome most challenges due to their experience, maturity, and communication skills. Your role now as a manager is to provide them the resources and political backing they need when asked. This is much different than the first two stages in which you functioned primarily as a supervisor. You fully empower your employees and then get out of the way while they make you look good. This is like handing off a football to a running back and watching him run.

The type of employees who operate in the Full Empowerment stage are your stars and really make coming to work so much easier. As I previously stated, having employees functioning in the last two stages will result in a high performance work unit. Many of these folks will likely be your future managers. This is where you want to hone their skills for leadership with the proper training plan and courses to help them advance toward management.

Training and Training Programs

This can be as deep or shallow of a subject as you would like it to be. A great deal of money is spent on training but how effective it is becomes the question. Most people forget the basic elements of the training class they took in only a week after they return to the job. What is the goal of the particular training? Chapter 6, "What Are We Trying to Solve Here?" contains the three basics of Strategic Management that I suggest be applied to the individual employee for training needs. They are:

1. **What are we trying to solve here?**

2. **Who are we going to impact?**

3. **Why are we doing this? (Specifically, what is the real requirement?)**

Ask these questions when you decide to send someone to training. Is it compulsory training that the organization requires? If so, then you comply but maybe not expect too much in the way of employee impact. If the training is simply to give them a break from the grind then you have your answer. However, for most employees you want to target their training to their particular professional development. Hence, let us apply the above criteria of the three basics of Strategic Management to meet their professional needs. For example, if the employee has difficulty in an area such as written communication, then you want to send them to a training class specifically to help them improve and eventually resolve that issue. That completes the first check in the box of what we are trying to solve? Next is, who are we going to impact? This is answered by the fact that the employee's customers, and you as the manager, are directly affected by an improved written communication ability. Third, why are we doing this? (Specifically, what is the real requirement)? If communication is a real requirement of the job, then we want the employee to improve this area of his/her performance. Essentially, that is how it is done. By using a process like this, you remove the ambiguity as to whether they should take this or that course, if it will help them, and you can afford to have them out of the office for x number of days, etc. These are all subjective questions that muddy the decision-making process.

Another example would be the training courses needed for the employee at the Full Empowerment stage who is functioning at a high level. Let's say you have identified them as one of your future managers and believe they would benefit from leadership training. In applying the three basics of Strategic Management again, you just answered the first question of what you are trying to solve, which is to help fill the internal management pipeline with future management candidates through targeted training. The next question of who are we going to impact is answered by your belief that this employee can be a contributor to the company as a potential manager. The third question of why are we doing this is answered by wanting to improve the leadership abilities within this individual so they will be better equipped to assume a management position in the future.

If you apply this technique, then you can save yourself time and effectively target training classes that will greatly assist your employees in their professional growth. You will also save your company training dollars that could be utilized elsewhere. No manager can defend a bloated training budget or a training budget with related travel that drives budgets even higher. Therefore, be selective in how you identify the training needed for your employees and the respective criteria you use. The bottom line is that you want to help them in their career if you can. In many organizations, especially in the public sector, employees are rarely afforded benefits outside of a salary and some vacation/sick days. Training may be one of the only rewards they receive and that a manager can provide them. Supporting your employees in this area goes a long way in demonstrating that you want to sow into them for the betterment of themselves and the company or organization that employs them.

CHAPTER 11

MEN AND WOMEN WORKFORCE DYNAMICS

No one wants to discuss this topic, but it needs to be addressed if you are going to be in management and want to be a successful manager. *What they should have told you in undergraduate or graduate school is that there is a difference between men and women when it comes to workplace dynamics.* People need to work together, and women are socially better at it than men due to their higher emotional IQ. They come into a work environment and look to relate to their surroundings and co-workers. They do not necessarily want to be placed in a cubicle and expected to function alone without communication. On the contrary, you have to be careful of placing a man into a cubicle to work independently on tasks. Men have the potential to remain there all day and never come out! Yes, work "man caves" do exist if you have not figured that out. That may be fine if it is what is required for the expected product, but probably is not as common in today's interconnected workforce.

Understanding Your Workforce Dynamics

When you inherit a group of employees in your management assignment, you first need to understand the dynamics of that particular group of people to conclude how the men and women work and function together. Does the team work well? Is it healthy and productive? Are they respectful to one another? Do they help or hinder each other getting the job done?

Workforce Diversity

Next, for both men and women managers, take a look at your staff and ask yourself if it is a balanced and diverse workforce. Does it reflect your industry population demographics? Do you have men and women in various positions throughout your staff, or does it look mostly one way or the other? Data shows that diversity increases productivity levels. I personally have hired and promoted more women and minorities than any of my counterparts. I did this not to prove a point or reach some sort of social quota, which I do not necessarily agree with as a concept. On the contrary, I actually stumbled onto the fact that diversity increases productivity levels. Now, industry data is supporting this conclusion which I unintentionally discovered. How did I arrive at this deduction? As a young manager, I made it a point to deliberately hire and promote the right person for the right job who was talented and showed potential. I call it the "right fit approach" because it was not necessarily the most intelligent or hardest worker that I would select to fill a position. It was about selecting the best person for that particular position. The one who possessed the right personality to go along with the other characteristics we were looking for in a candidate to complement our team and where we were heading. I have written more about this in Chapter 9, "Hiring/Staffing."

I believe this right fit approach was fostered out of my college experience and then reinforced by different readings focused on looking for the inherent giftedness of the individual in job matching/placement and not simply intelligence and ability. In conjunction, I flashed back to my undergraduate days and remembered comments made by some fellow classmates during our senior year that always stuck with me. Specifically, there were two individuals in particular who had the highest grade point average (GPA) among our engineering class. They believed that being smart and having the highest GPA made them superior and were the only things needed to get the best paying jobs coming out of college. No hiring manager would dare refuse them. That always stuck with me because these same people, one man and one woman, could be obnoxious and hard to be around let alone work with. Nevertheless, the smartest person may not necessarily be the best fit for your work unit.

When there were discussions on staffing and turnover issues in the organizations I worked for, I used to sincerely state to HR and my manager colleagues that I had the United Nations working for me and believed that should be the model. Anyone could look across my workforce and see different genders, races, and ethnicities filling management and non-management positions. It was balanced and healthier than most work areas wherever I managed. As a direct consequence, my staff's productivity levels were higher as well. All of the managers knew about the EEO policies to be followed, but for some reason many departments hired the same type of people that thought alike and even looked very similar to one another. This hiring approach eventually hurts the company/organization in the long run due to minimal divergent opinions from the lack of diversity.

Women in Management

A major issue affecting women in management is with regard to attaining that first level management position.[1] It is not due to encountering the proverbial glass ceiling. The glass ceiling metaphor was coined many decades ago and tends to be used when identifying the hidden barriers keeping women from advancing to the upper management ranks. In this situation though, it appears to be more of an "initial barrier" in reaching that first rung of a woman's career ladder than it does a glass ceiling, since it is the first stage of moving into the management ranks.[1] Sometimes, it has also been referred to as the "sticky floor," meaning holding a group of people back by keeping them at the bottom of the workforce in entry-level type positions.

In providing some background on this issue, it should be made clear that the number of men and women entering the U.S. labor force are about the same. From there, and contrary to some beliefs, data shows that women have just as much desire to be in management as men. However, around 40% of women believe they are judged by different standards when it comes to being placed in management.[1] Whether that is true or not, it is a perception that must be taken into consideration. When it comes to attaining that first management position in a woman's career ladder, the latest 2019 study by McKinsey & Company and LeanIn.org contains a revealing statistic. Women have around a 42% rate of placement into first level management jobs compared to their male counterparts who are just above the 58% mark. That number appears to be steady since 2015.[3] Furthermore, this imbalance can be even greater in certain industries such as health care and customer service where the entry or junior level workforce is predominantly made up of women, but men occupy the majority of the management positions. These "inversion" type settings appear to be a long-standing trend in these types of industries.[1]

Overcoming the Initial Barrier

So why is this initial barrier of women achieving that first level management position so important? Follow me with this analogy. I remember when planning to take the SAT and GMAT tests for college admissions, we were told that if a person missed the first couple of questions on the exam then it would dramatically affect their overall score. Regardless if a person answered most of the remaining questions correctly, they could never overcome the effects of that first missed opportunity so early in the exam. Similarly, the long-term effects of the lower rate of women entering into first management level positions is a missed opportunity that sets the stage for reduced numbers of women filling upper management positions later. Bottom line, they can never catch up similar to the SAT/GMAT test score analogy. Currently, that is a major reason why you can look around a department head meeting or an executive boardroom and see mostly men sitting in those chairs. Gender diversity cannot solely exist at the senior management ranks or else it looks suspect. It has to be throughout the company or organization for true diversity to take shape, take hold, and make a difference. The last few years, employers are supporting programs that attempt to promote and insert women into upper management positions. However, the lower management positions do not appear to be getting the same attention even though that is the first critical step of the proverbial career ladder and THE feeder or pipeline to fill those upper management positions. To overcome this dilemma, women even more than men have to take control of their own career and plot their path to that first level management position within their company or organization. They have to be somewhat assertive and let their current management know they aspire to the role of manager. Specifically, they need to request their supervisor's support to help them overcome any apparent weaknesses that are holding them back from attaining that initial management position. Next, they need to lay out a plan to achieve that goal and get their supervisor to review it, approve it, and support it. As a result, a women's career ladder may look different than their male counterparts as they begin their entry into management, but it can be just as effective if not more so in the long run.

Who's Your Sea Daddy?

Women, as well as men, need someone within their company or organization to believe in them and be their champion as they vie for advancement to that first management position in their career ladder. I like the old school expression that was used in the U.S. Navy in which a junior ranked person is supposed to have a "Sea Daddy" who helps them along early in their career and shows them the ropes, so to speak. (Note: A "Sea Daddy" can be either a man or woman of higher rank in the U.S. Navy).

Important personnel decisions are quite often made behind closed doors by managers. As an aspiring manager, you probably will not be present in the room to defend yourself or sell your skills and abilities for that particular upcoming hot project or management position. You need someone internally who can advocate for you and who knows you professionally. That person is able to influence some of the key decision makers in your company and be your champion. In life as well as business, you cannot do it alone regardless of what you have been told and no matter how driven you are. The terms "self-made man" and "self-made woman" are very deceitful. They imply that a person was virtually unassisted in successfully arriving at their current status in life. That is ridiculous. John Donne's famous poem *No Man Is An Island* should be read and contemplated if one even possesses a smidgen of this attitude. Bottom line, find yourself a Sea Daddy!

Positioning Is Important

Many times, women may encumber positions that do not possess much upward mobility.[1] We call them dead-end jobs, which can cause someone in a support role to remain there. As I noted in Chapter 8, "Understanding and Handling Employee Turnover," men and women leave their jobs at around the same rate and at every stage of a career — from entry level to manager to senior manager, etc. all the way up to the corporate suite executive positions. Without getting into mandated quotas, how women are positioned to succeed may make all the difference when moving up the career ladder towards upper management positions.[2] Specifically, this is critical when hiring a person with a lot of upside potential but placing them in a limited position with a constrained role. (I talk about this in Chapter 9, "Hiring/Staffing," in the "Job Fit and Future" section.) They will never have the opportunity to flourish as a result.

Well Qualified

It is important in any company or organization to create a feeder, or pipeline, of viable candidates for upper management ranks. From a long-term perspective, when the gender disparity in first level management begins to close by inserting more women into those positions, it will have a major effect on women filling more senior management positions. Then the pipeline will be more plentiful with qualified women candidates vying for increased levels of responsibility and prominence instead of being left behind. Accordingly, one important factor that rings true is that women need to ensure they are well qualified to be in the pipeline. This helps to set them apart from the other employees contending for a management job. Women have to consistently perform at a high level - not only to be considered for management but more importantly, to be able to succeed when the stress and strain of the management position begins to weigh on them as it does for anyone who serves in the management ranks.

Prove Thyself

Female managers can feel the need to prove themselves more so than their male counterparts. If a woman is not secure in herself, she can let her insecurities affect her employees by directing apprehensions toward them. This is especially true of her junior female employees who are subject to experiencing jealousies about their youth and abilities. Do not let this happen if you are a woman who desires to become a manager. As I say in Chapter 13, "Be Honest with Yourself and Grow," you will eventually be placed in a management position for a reason. Therefore, do it justice and be an example of a professional who operates in an unbiased manner. Regardless of your gender, never use your position of authority to harm someone. Also, be careful not to show gender favoritism in hiring, promoting, and job assignments. As a male manager, be careful not to embrace the "good ole boy" mentality as a characteristic of your management style. Furthermore, do not hire, promote, and assign the good tasks only to people who are just like you. For example, I had an older woman who worked for me as a division manager. She had been with the company for many years and was very capable and hard working. One day my director approached me and asked for my hands-on involvement in her hiring practices. I was recently hired into the workplace and therefore could provide objectivity. He identified to me a concerning trend that this division manager was hiring people who were just like her. Furthermore, he went on to say that her employees were quiet like church mice and would only do what she told them to do. When I took inventory of her workforce, I found that was indeed true. She hired mostly females who were quiet individuals who would not challenge her in any way. Otherwise, she put them in their place. This practice not only hurt the employees, but it hurt the department. Unfortunately, no innovation or fresh thinking ever came out of this manager's area. Mostly compliance-type work was ever produced. After I began sitting on the hiring panels with her, we were able to select men and women with good talent who were not afraid to challenge the norm and produce results. This was uncomfortable for her, but she needed to grow as a manager and as a person. The only way for that to happen was for her to be stretched outside her comfort zone, which is usually a "control zone" for many people when you really think about it. That freaks them out! This sort of change usually requires extra "care and feeding," as the saying goes, by the next higher-level manager. In this case, I was that manager. I had to help guide her down the path while presenting a safe environment for her to embrace a new mindset that what was now expected of her by me.

JOHN BALESTRIERI

Providing Performance Feedback to Men and Women

How should you provide performance feedback to men and women who work for you? Any anticipated confrontation is not comfortable for anyone in a management position. No one truly enjoys it. However, when it comes to employee feedback, there has to be a level of it for the manager to effectively guide or recalibrate the performance of his staff. It does get easier as you become more experienced as a manager. This naturally occurs from all of the interactions you obtain during the many performance reviews you administer. These reviews may be the only time in which you can sit down uninterrupted with each staff member and assess their performance in a direct way. Make the "D and D" approach (detailed/direct) be part of your performance feedback style. Be detailed and be direct to both your men and women employees.[4] Specifically, be detailed when initially setting their performance goals to rule out being nebulous in your expectations. Likewise, be direct in providing feedback for the results you are looking for compared to the goals that were set at the beginning of the performance cycle. This will eliminate generic feedback assessments. Finally, be detailed when you provide your feedback as to what they have done well and what they need to improve upon.

There is a difference in the "D and D" approach between being direct/detailed versus nitpicking/critical. Keep an eye on that. You, as the manager, will have to get over any stigma of being too harsh by giving constructive feedback to men and especially women. Women deserve the same quality of input by their rating manager as men. There is no need to have dichotomies in your range of directness — either being too harsh or too soft. There is an in between ground, or as they say in baseball, a "sweet spot," that you will find when providing feedback. Believe it or not, employees will realize and understand your rhythm of doing things and work with you if they believe you are genuine in your intent toward them.

Speaking of baseball, I sometimes like to put the ball in an employee's field of play during the first and last part of the performance feedback session and ask them questions. This gets them to open up and not feel apprehensive as if they were called to the principal's office. I may start the performance review with the first two questions below from an overall perspective and then afterward ask about specific elements being observed in their performance plan. Then, I like to conclude with the last two questions of the feedback session. I interact with them in each of these questions:

1. **"How do you think you did overall during this (performance) cycle?"**

2. **"Could you have done anything better?"** (This is where you can offer specific feedback if there was an element that would help them to grow.)

3. **"Are there any areas that you think you want to target for growth?"** (This lets you know about their self-awareness and potential.)

4. **"What do you need from me going into the next cycle?"**

Remember to be an active listener during the performance feedback reviews especially when the employee states what they need help with or if they ask about opportunities for growth within the company. Hearing them talk will give you insights into their future fit with the company.

The Equity Concept

As I have addressed the topic of women in first level management positions earlier in the chapter, I would like to emphasize that I am not advocating for quotas. It is quite the opposite. I would like to balance that notion with a somewhat radical concept that could be career and life changing if you allow it to be. Too much has been made of equality in the workforce, and I believe it has caused the real goal to be lost along the way. What is really needed is "equity" in the workforce. I call this the equity concept. We need to stop comparing ourselves with another person regardless of their gender, race, age, title, pay, etc. in an attempt to be equal with them on some scale. This leads to striving and resentment when a person feels they are coming up short in areas of importance to them. Instead, embrace the differences in how you and they are made. Look to be compensated for what you bring to the company or organization that employs you. Look for equity! You will always find someone in life who is taller, better looking, more intelligent, better educated, more successful, earns a higher salary, etc. Have you ever met someone (outside your work environment) who made a lot more money than you but was less talented in many areas and you wondered, "How is that possible?" You may have even blurted out, "That's not fair!" Well, if all things were equal then you are correct, it's not fair. What is occurring here is the equity concept. The skills and abilities the individual does have are being utilized in an opportune (right) venue for them to thrive. Thus, they are being successful and well-rewarded as a result.

Trying to be equal with anyone will rob you of who you really are. If there are characteristics of a person that you admire or simply are appealing, then it is perfectly OK to attempt to incorporate those into your repertoire as a growth mechanism but not an identity stealer. Let's face it, where you are now as a person and professional is a result of many influencers (people) who have been part of your life over the years. Try to see beyond the apparent disparities in the workplace that are supposed to offend you when things look unfair. Go deeper within yourself to be better than you should be instead of only expecting to be made equal with someone. After that, if you cannot get the equity you deserve in your workplace then move on to something better and somewhere better if there is no outlook for a positive change. This includes gender pay inequity that exists in the marketplace. Go to where you are valued!

Obtaining Value in the Equity Concept

I was profoundly affected by this next story that reinforces the equity concept. I worked with a person a few years ago who was highly educated and good at his profession. He was in an established position that had a direct impact on an important area of our organization but was not given a lot of notoriety. He was certainly not looking for it. However, he felt constrained by top management who placed limitations on his empowerment even though he was the proven expert with many years of experience in his field. They had their opinions, but if they would just trust and empower him more, he could show greater results with widespread impacts. Years went by. Then one day he received a phone call from a company that heard about what he was doing and how it could benefit their vision and workforce. He was shocked to receive the call and that they even knew who he was. At first, he was not open to talking with them and did not want to leave our organization. He liked the city he lived in and the family situation he had at that time in his life. However, they asked for a meeting with him, and he reluctantly obliged. During the meeting, the management team explained their vision and how he fit into where their company was headed. They talked about how his work and abilities would be valuable to their organization and its employees. They valued him to the point where they gladly accommodated his work/life balance requests and offered him four times his current salary without any negotiations! I remember talking with him prior to his departure to this new company. He said that the money part was nice but not his primary motivation to leave the organization in which he invested many years. He was a person of principle who realized the value he had to offer and his motivation factors were different. Ultimately, his deciding factor to leave was when he realized he was valued more by an outside organization than by his own. That last sentence is my point in a nutshell. He got his equity.

By the way, the equity concept can be used in your non-work life relationships, especially those who are looking for marriage in their future. In any relationship, both parties bring their own strengths and weaknesses to the table. No one has the complete 100% package that you should somehow expect to be equal with. You bring just as much to the table that gives you the "equity" and confidence you need to hold your own with anyone regardless of who they are. This concept of equity may be a tough one to grab hold of. However, if you can do it, then it can be liberating to the point that it sets you free to soar to new heights!

CHAPTER 12

WORKING WITH OR IN A MILITARY CULTURE

If you are going to work in the Department of Defense (DOD) as a DOD employee or Defense contractor then you will be thrust into a military culture with all of its idiosyncrasies. In order to successfully function in this environment, it is necessary to understand the paradigm of the military trained leadership with whom you will be interacting. The U.S. military services rotate their personnel on short-term assignments from location to location typically on a two to three-year cycle. The U.S. Air Force has the longest rotation length, which can be up to five years. The purpose of these assignments is to develop their personnel, specifically the commissioned and noncommissioned officers, providing hands-on experience with increasing levels of responsibilities and sphere of influence with the intent to increase their leadership ability.

Officer Personnel

For the officer ranks, each duty assignment is referred to as "checking the block" on their way to advancement to the next promotion level. Officers are the white-collar managers of the military and begin their career at the O-1 level. The "O" is for officer, and they progress to the next alphanumeric level, O-2, O-3, O-4, etc., on a time-based system with acceptable performance. See Table 1.[1] They will usually achieve the O-5 level without a problem by their 20 years of service. That equates to being a Commander in the U.S. Navy/Coast Guard or a Lieutenant Colonel in the other branches of services. To reach the O-6 level, which is a Navy/Coast Guard Captain or Colonel rank, it is much more competitive but achievable. Those who excel in leadership will ensure they check all those blocks to include completing the more difficult assignments to impress the promotion review board. Those who have the right supportive headship looking over them will achieve the O-6 rank. For those officers at this juncture, the military is definitely their career and way of life. After that rank is reached, the possibility exists to achieve the O-7 level or higher, which is the General or Admiral level, i.e. General Officer/Flag Officer (GOFO) as it is called. However, the GOFO level is very political, even in the military. Furthermore, the higher a person aspires for promotion, the more they discover they must adjust their temperament in order to navigate the political channels. Personal trade-offs and sometimes personality trade-offs must be made as one climbs higher in rank. Some do this better than others.

RANK INSIGNIA OF THE U.S. ARMED FORCES

ENLISTED

	E-1	E-2	E-3	E-4	E-5	E-6	E-7	E-8	E-9
ARMY	no insignia — Private E-1 (PV1)	Private (PV2)	Private First Class (PFC)	Specialist (SPC) / Corporal (CPL)	Sergeant (SGT)	Staff Sergeant (SSG)	Sergeant First Class (SFC)	Master Sergeant (MSG) / First Sergeant (1SG)	Sergeant Major (SGM) / Command Sergeant Major (CSM) / Sergeant Major of the Army (SMA)
MARINES	no insignia — Private (Pvt)	Private First Class (PFC)	Lance Corporal (LCpl)	Corporal (Cpl)	Sergeant (Sgt)	Staff Sergeant (SSgt)	Gunnery Sergeant (GySgt)	Master Sergeant (MSgt) / First Sergeant (1stSgt)	Master Gunnery Sergeant (MGySgt) / Sergeant Major (SgtMaj) / Sergeant Major of the Marine Corps (SgtMajMC)
AIR FORCE	no insignia — Airman Basic (AB)	Airman (Amn)	Airman First Class (A1C)	Senior Airman (SrA)	Staff Sergeant (SSgt)	Technical Sergeant (TSgt)	Master Sergeant (MSgt)	Senior Master Sergeant (SMSgt)	Chief Master Sergeant (CMSgt) / Command Chief Master Sergeant (CCM/CMSgt) / Chief Master Sergeant of the Air Force (CMSAF)
NAVY	no insignia — Seaman Recruit (SR)	Seaman Apprentice (SA)	Seaman (SN)	Petty Officer Third Class (PO3)	Petty Officer Second Class (PO2)	Petty Officer First Class (PO1)	Chief Petty Officer (CPO)	Senior Chief Petty Officer (SCPO)	Master Chief Petty Officer (MCPO) / Force or Fleet Master Chief Petty Officer (FORMC/FLTMC) / Master Chief Petty Officer of the Navy (MCPON)
COAST GUARD	no insignia — Seaman Recruit (SR)	Seaman Apprentice (SA)	Seaman (SN)	Petty Officer Third Class (PO3)	Petty Officer Second Class (PO2)	Petty Officer First Class (PO1)	Chief Petty Officer (CPO)	Senior Chief Petty Officer (SCPO)	Master Chief Petty Officer (MCPO) / Command Master Chief Officer (CMC) / Master Chief Petty Officer of the Coast Guard (MCPO-CG)

RANK INSIGNIA OF THE U.S. ARMED FORCES

OFFICERS

	O-1	O-2	O-3	O-4	O-5	O-6	O-7	O-8	O-9	O-10	SPECIAL
ARMY · AIR FORCE · MARINES	Second Lieutenant (2LT)	First Lieutenant (1LT)	Captain (CPT)	Major (MAJ)	Lieutenant Colonel (LTC)	Colonel (COL)	Brigadier General (BG)	Major General (MG)	Lieutenant General (LTG)	General (GEN)	General of the Army (GA)
NAVY · COAST GUARD	Ensign (ENS)	Lieutenant Junior Grade (LTJG)	Lieutenant (LT)	Lieutenant Commander (LCDR)	Commander (CDR)	Captain (CAPT)	Rear Admiral Lower Half (RADM(LH))	Rear Admiral Upper Half (RADM(UH))	Vice Admiral (VADM)	Admiral (ADM)	Fleet Admiral (FADM)

Warrant Officers

	W-1	W-2	W-3	W-4	W-5
ARMY	Warrant Officer 1 (WO1)	Chief Warrant Officer (CW2)	Chief Warrant Officer (CW3)	Chief Warrant Officer (CW4)	Chief Warrant Officer (CW5)
NAVY · COAST GUARD	Warrant Officer 1 (WO1)*	Chief Warrant Officer (CWO2)	Chief Warrant Officer (CWO3)	Chief Warrant Officer (CWO4)	Chief Warrant Officer (CWO5)
MARINES	Warrant Officer (WO)	Chief Warrant Officer (CWO2)	Chief Warrant Officer (CWO3)	Chief Warrant Officer (CWO4)	Chief Warrant Officer (CWO5)
AIR FORCE	NO WARRANT	NO WARRANT	NO WARRANT	NO WARRANT	NO WARRANT
COAST GUARD					No Chief Warrant Officer (CWO5)

* The grade of Warrant Officer W-1 is no longer in use.

Officer Education Requirements

Officers are initially required to have formal higher education with a four-year degree and then an advanced degree as they promote to the upper military ranks. There are different ways to become a commissioned officer. One way is by attending one of the three Service academies for the Navy (and Marine Corp), Army, Air Force. The Coast Guard is part of the Department of Homeland Security and has its own academy. These are all accredited four-year universities that require official nomination by a student's local congressional representative for consideration to be accepted. At these academies the individuals take undergraduate courses like they would at any other college or university but with a heavy emphasis on leadership, military tactics, and their respective military occupation specialty that they decide to be employed after graduation. This educational experience is funded by the U.S. taxpayers and will require the accepted student to fulfill at least a four-year active duty or six-year reserve duty obligation of service once they graduate and are commissioned as an O-1. The annual cost of education per student is over $250,000. When was the last time you were given a "thank you" by an academy graduate, Mr. and Mrs. Taxpayer?

The United States Naval Academy is located in Annapolis, Maryland, and allows its graduates to be commissioned as officers in the United States Navy/Navy Reserve or United States Marine Corps/Reserve. The United States Military Academy is located in West Point, New York, and allows its graduates to be commissioned as officers in the United States Army/Reserve. The United States Air Force Academy is located in Colorado Springs, Colorado, and allows its graduates to be commissioned as officers in the United States Air Force/Reserve. The United States Coast Guard Academy is located in New London,

Connecticut, and allows its graduates to be commissioned as officers in the United States Coast Guard/Reserve. Graduates of these Academies are considered professionals and unofficially afforded what is called the "fast track" to reach the O-6 rank. They also are normally the leaders who run the military services at the highest levels. The nickname for Academy graduates is "ring knockers" and the way you can identify them is by their Service Academy college ring they wear on their right forefinger.

The next way to become a military officer is to already possess a four-year undergraduate degree and then apply to the Officer Candidate School (OCS) of one of the military services. OCS was used extensively during World War II, and that is how the name "90-day wonder" came about. A person would enter this type of boot camp for aspiring officers on day 1 and on day 90 they would be commissioned in their respective military service officer ranks as an O-1.

The final way to become a military officer is to be accepted into a Reserve Officer Training Corps (ROTC) while attending a college or university. ROTC is a college and university-based training program that allows a student to choose their own scholastic field of study but with military courses added in. Upon graduation with a four-year degree, the graduate is commissioned as an O-1 into the branch of service for the ROTC program they selected. Many of these ROTC programs will pay for the last two years of the individual's schooling and this obligates them to a four-year direct officer commission in the military or a six-year officer commission in the active reserves.

Enlisted Personnel

For the enlisted personnel, their ranking structure ranges from E-1 to E-9. The "E" stands for "enlisted." Once a service member reaches the E-6 rank, they are comparable to a blue-collar supervisor/foreman in the private sector. As they move up the enlisted ranks, they are given increasing levels in responsibility and direct supervision over the junior enlisted personnel assigned to them. This continues all the way up until the E-9 level. However, similar to any promotional pyramid system, there are fewer opportunities as the rank increases. It becomes much more competitive to reach the E-8 and E-9 ranks. These levels are usually the Master Sergeant, Sergeant Major, Senior Chief, and Master Chief titles. Formal higher education is not officially required as an enlisted member. However, it is advantageous, especially when there is a need to show separation among their peers as they look to be promoted to the upper echelons and become a non-commissioned officer, which is the E-7, E-8, and E-9 ranks.

When an individual enters the United States military as an enlisted person, they are required to sign a contract between themselves and the United States government for a specified period. It is usually a four-year contract unless some additional entitlements are provided to the individual such as extended schooling or financial bonuses. For example, people wanting nuclear training are called "Nukes" and will usually have to sign a six-year contact. The reason for this is that their provided schooling alone is two years and may contain a $40,000 enlistment bonus. Therefore, for the government to recoup their training investment made in the individual, they will require four years of work following the completion of their training cycle. As that six-year contract reaches culmination, the service member has the ability to earn a $100,000 reenlistment bonus if they want to remain in that military field. Then they will have to sign another contract for four years of service. Not too shabby if you are a Nuke, Submariner, IT specialist, etc. working in one of those specialized military disciplines and can garner that type of entitlement!

Military Officers – Their Style

Military officers, by personality, are type A and aggressive. ISTJ's (Myers/Briggs) personality types are considered the perfect match for these officer positions. Their training teaches them to be aggressive and overcome obstacles. "Adapt and overcome" is the trademark of the military culture. Therefore, you have to understand this basic fundamental when working with or for them. Most officers are reasonable, levelheaded people. However, make no mistake that their focus is to get the job done and accomplish the mission.

Many individuals who work with military officers on a regular basis can get steamrolled by what is perceived as a bully approach. If this occurs, they are simply following their engrained training as an officer, and you have to be careful not to be offended or intimidated. They will push, push, push to get what they want or think they need. This is true for the non-commissioned officer ranks as well. You need to recognize this mannerism when interacting with them. It will help you know how to respond to their demands and if necessary, push back as well. Keep in mind that they are evaluated every year on their performance by their superiors with what is called a Fitness Report (FITREP). This FITREP will be is used to support their selection for their next promotion and duty assignment/location. They do not want to fail or be ranked as simply satisfactory by their rating official so they will look to "accomplish their mission" by achieving their work assignments that may involve your area of responsibility. They have skin in the game, more or less. The bad part is that it usually takes them about eight months to a year to become savvy in the job they are placed. Then they are transitioning out of that job the last two months of their two-year rotation cycle. That leaves roughly 12 months of potential effectiveness they will have in any job to be able to excel with an outside chance of making change. This fact is very evident to them and sometimes frustrating as well since they will be dealing with a civilian workforce who will remain there on an enduring basis. They may see these civilians as either an aid or detriment to what they expect to achieve. The good part is that they bring a fresh external perspective when they come to an organization along with a level of professionalism and motivation, which can be contagious.

I have found most military officers are good people who are very committed when it comes to their duties. There are exceptions. Some do take the aggressive part a little too far and do not embrace the reality of their bureaucratic organization with its limitations in getting the job done. Conversely, this is exactly the demeanor we want of them when deployed to a hostile area of the world or on the battlefield. However, it has its drawbacks in an office setting with civilian and contractor employees. Many times, the military officer struggles to understand the rules that have been established by Congress and the government system they are a part of. They also can be oblivious to the fact that once they depart the organization after their assignment is completed, the civilian and contractor workforce has to function within the policies or processes that they created or changed and live with the consequences. Their predominance to a leadership mindset many times dwarfs the practical aspects of successfully operating in a non-tactical, non-deployed environment such as a policy or resourcing headquarters consisting of military, civilian, and contract employees. The "adapt and overcome" trademark I mentioned earlier in the chapter is oftentimes minus the adapt part and just "let's overcome" the situation or roadblock on the way to achieving the goal. This can be costly, especially when there is law, rules, and policy that must be adhered to. I cannot recall how many times I have had to explain these facts to military officers who just wanted to steamroll everyone and everything on the way to the finish line. It was as though the issue they were working had never been attempted before and the rest of us should just "get in line" to ensure their expectation was met. I share this with you so that when you are in these types of situations, you will know what to expect and be able to react accordingly.

Getting to Yes (with COAs)

"Getting to yes" is a popular saying by the military when they want something and know there are impediments to achieving that goal. What you have to do in these situations is understand where they are coming from and show that you are willing to assist them even if it is in a way they have not thought about. During any meetings, be careful how you respond so that you do not come across as a complete "no" to their request if possible. Sometimes, "no" is not a dirty word insomuch as how it is relayed to the other party. Provide them courses of action (COAs), which is military speak for the way they like to decide a situation. These COAs are usually in a PowerPoint presentation that consists of three solutions from which they can choose. They should be legal and within policy of course. The first COA is what you want them to select. The second COA is a compromise but not optimal and only gets them to a certain point. The last COA is a throw away due to its severity that no one wants for a solution. If you can do what I am suggesting above, you will build their trust and respect because they see your character and willingness to work with them.

When in meetings with multiple stakeholders and the situation or discussion becomes more volatile, try not to escalate things. Specifically, never embarrass or show up a military officer or upper ranking enlisted person in front of others. Even if they are wrong, point to the facts and steer them to the solution you believe is best or optimal for the issue at hand. In these instances, I encourage you to go to the military officer off-line and talk it over with them. Many situations have been deescalated and resolved by an offline meeting in the officer's office via the one-on-one approach. Once they can see your perspective and how it will help them succeed, they will come around. This will go a long way in your working relationship with them especially when you are in future meetings or have to collaborate on projects. Always remember to operate by the old leadership axiom, which is to reward in public but reprimand in private.

By the way, the world is small. *What they should have told you in undergraduate or graduate school is not to be surprised if you encounter that same military leader (or any other manager for that sake) later on in your work career at a higher rank or position of authority.* They will remember how you dealt with them and handled yourself. Consequently, those dividends will pay off in the next phase of your work life with them. I can attest to this personally.

CHAPTER 13

BE HONEST WITH YOURSELF AND GROW

For most people, one of the toughest things to do in life is possess self-awareness. It can be defined as the ability to realize who you are on the inside and then improve those areas that you want or need to grow and mature. To be truly honest with yourself as both a person and a professional is to be able to make the appropriate internal adjustments on how you think and act.

Emotional Intelligence

Emotional intelligence or emotional IQ is becoming more of a popular concept these days. The term was coined by Peter Salovey and John Mayer in the 1990s. They describe it as "a form of social intelligence that involves the ability to monitor one's own and other's feelings and emotions, to discriminate among them, and to use this information to guide one's thinking and action."[1] It links directly to overall self-awareness as a key component for you as a professional and person in order to grow and mature. I believe the more self-aware you are, the higher the probability of having an increased emotional IQ. In 1998, Daniel Goleman further defined Salovey and Mayer's work into four characteristics or categories:[1]

Self-awareness – Awareness of your own emotions

Self-management – Ability to control your own emotions through recognition and response

Social awareness – Empathy for others with the ability to recognize their emotions

Social Skills (relationship management) – Ability to manage other people's emotions in a meaningful way

Goleman believed emotional intelligence was the driving factor of a leader's business success and not cognitive intelligence. In fact, recent studies show a 75%/25% relationship of emotional intelligence/cognitive intelligence for leadership success.[2] However, it all starts with self-awareness. If you can achieve that goal, then the remaining three characteristics/categories of emotional intelligent leadership are fully attainable. The reason is if you know yourself, then you can manage your emotions better, are more aware of other people's emotions, and can interact with people in a meaningful way for a positive relationship.

Let me give you an example. When I first went into management,

I was inserted into a second-level management position as I mentioned previously. I did not have the luxury to begin my career as a first-line supervisor. I was a division manager over four branches with a supervisor in charge of each branch. There was one supervisor in particular who drove me crazy with his style and mannerisms. He was smart and clever, maybe too much for his own good. But that is the reason he was promoted into first-level management. However, once in the supervisor position, he would often become lazy or laisse-faire in how he managed. He accomplished the job, but not the way I would have done it. I truly believed the problem was with him and not me. Then one weekend I was enlightened. I was invited to an event where the speaker discussed personality types and used a quad chart to explain how people roughly fall into four basic categories, which in essence drives their behavior. In addition, there were no right or wrong personality types. This was my initial exposure to this type of information. As I sat attentively listening, I began to realize who I was and then was able to better understand who this subordinate manager of mine was as well. This moved me into the self-awareness phase, which is the first emotional IQ characteristic mentioned earlier. I returned to work with a reduced sense of frustration in managing him and the rest of my managers and employees for that matter. This ushered me into the self-management phase of the emotional IQ characteristics. I had a greater appreciation for his abilities and empathy for who he was. This moved me into the social awareness phase, which is the third emotional IQ characteristic. Then I gave him the freedom to be himself more, and he took care of me as a result, always getting the job done. This moved me into the social skills (or relationship management) phase of the emotional IQ characteristics. The crazy thing about all of it was that this subordinate manager and I went from butting heads to working well together and eventually becoming friends who respected each other.

Keep in mind, I still set the vision and goals for the division, but I let go of the need to control how it all got accomplished. This overall self-awareness first caused me to realize who I was, make the appropriate corrections within myself, become more socially aware of others (without judging them), and then positively affect those relationships around me. This is how it should work. It is a four-step process. I went from being an autocratic-type leader to one who empowered his workforce. This benefitted both the organization and the employees. Productivity increased along with morale all because I was open-minded and willing to be honest with myself and grow. I have since discovered more in-depth personality profiles such as the widely known Myers-Briggs Type Indicator for example, that have improved my awareness in this area.

Who Checks You?

Many times, I have asked the hard question, "Who checks you?" Meaning, who has permission or access to your life and who knows you well enough to tell you the truth about your actions? Most people do not have or allow this type of relationship. No one wants to be told they are "off-base" or "missing it" in their professional or personal lives. To admit this, means we may have a sort of character flaw. It could also infer that we are not in control as much as we thought and probably have failed in those areas. Yet for someone to tell us these things and to "check us" is exactly what we need. For myself, having this type of relationship with a friend who can understand my work life and personal life has made a world of difference. As a result, I have grown as person, a manager, and a leader. I am now able to catch myself when I start to get off track in an area and can shine the light on my own motives and actions. These are the self-awareness and self-management characteristics of emotional intelligence. Then I can honestly access the "why" in what I am doing. I currently still allow those one or two relationships to provide me feedback. However, I believe the best case is to self-evaluate the "why" in what I do, as my set default.

These types of changes are huge in a person's life. They help you become a better manager, leader, and person. I always say that if you do not have children at home to develop you, then having employees at work will do many of the same things in their respective ways. You will be tried and tested by their attitudes and actions, which will cause you to react in one way or another. My blood pressure used to be high until I was forced to realize that I must be doing something wrong to continue to react in a less than positive way internally, and sometimes externally, in my communication with my workforce. Keep in mind that YOU are your greatest critic and greatest helper to improve your life as a manager. Allow one or two trusted confidants access to your professional and personal life and give them the freedom to provide you feedback and "check you," in specific work situations and mindsets you may have. Ask them this simple question after you have explained a particular work challenge or situation you are going through, "Am I off-base in how I am seeing this dilemma, or am I on track?" Try to be objective in painting the background of the issue by providing the other point of view, if you can do this. Then, let them give you feedback without retaliation. The benefits are extraordinary.

The practice of being checked by someone ultimately becomes paramount in a career and should be used often, especially when you are deciding to leave your company or organization for another one. There have been too many times when I have talked with employees who wanted to leave their company in looking for a promotion because they mistakenly believed they were better performers than what they really were. But once again, who "checks" them to help understand what the truth actually looks like in their life? The worst thing is for a person to remain self-deceived and carry that mindset into their next position at another company. *What they should have told you in undergraduate or graduate school is that pride is always the biggest obstacle to both personal and professional growth.* With a healthy dose of it, we can overcome and attain great heights. Conversely, with too large a dose of pride, we veer off into areas that can be detrimental thus affecting our decision-making. This can inevitably cause us pain and suffering since the only voice we tend to listen to and regard is our own. Don't be that guy! Be better than that.

Regardless of our age, we can always learn and evolve in our emotional intelligence and should do so in the different stages of our lives. Those who are older can definitely attest to this. Time has a way of seasoning us. Keep in mind that if you will not allow someone access into your life to provide input for your emotional growth, then failure will be your teacher and difficulties your companion. It will not be the circumstance, situation, or other person who is the problem in your immediate life. It will be the one who is looking back at you in the mirror each morning who is your problem. Take it from me, it is much better to learn from other people's mistakes, their wisdom, and their honest critique. So, be open to input from a trusted confidant. Be honest with yourself and grow.

CHAPTER 14

DO THE LITTLE THINGS TO SEPARATE YOURSELF

I try to tell young employees especially, "Do the little things to separate yourself from the rest of the pack." In baseball, every player would like to hit a grand slam homerun during each ballgame, but it does not work that way. Baseball is a game made up of singles and doubles, basic fundamentals, and a lot of other non-glamourous little things in between. However, that is how success and winning comes about in any sport. It is not talent alone, but the little things done well that separate the average players from the good players. All of them possess natural skills and abilities or else they would not be at that level. However, some seem to rise a little higher than the others do. It is the same in business. You will be working alongside bright and talented people. Many of those individuals possess their own drive, ambition, and expectations, but they can easily remain with the pack instead of separating themselves from it. *What they should have told you in undergraduate or graduate school is that differentiating oneself in the workplace is important and is achieved by having a sense of excellence, which is uncommon these days.* Whatever we do in the non-technical areas of our professional life should be done well regardless if they are considered major or minor things.

So what little things can be done to cause you to stand out from the rest and foster a manner of excellence? Allow me to focus on the basics first and then be overarching.

Basics:

- Be on time for work.

- Return from lunch on time.

- Respond to phone messages in a timely manner.

- Respond to emails in a timely manner.

- Leave out-of-office messages on your email and voicemail.

- Follow-up on action items from earlier meeting(s) in which tasked.

- Meet all work deadlines. Communicate and negotiate early on if due dates are unattainable.

- Spell-check your write-ups, presentations, and emails.

- Write mostly in an active voice instead of passive voice.

- Practice your presentations before going live in order to make adjustments and validate the flow.

- When giving presentations, use the three B's:

    Be Brief!

    Be Brilliant!

    Be Gone!

- Keep a log of your accomplishments throughout the year to place on your performance assessment.

- Be courteous when you talk with your customers.

- Compliment your co-workers when they have done something well.

- Compliment your staff when they have done something well.

- Verbally praise an employee in public.

- Verbally reprimand an employee in private.

- Do not use foul language when addressing your employees. Stay professional regardless of the situation.

- Demonstrate poise and composure to your staff when there is calamity and uncertainty. (If their leader is calm, they will follow suit.)

- Be punctual for meetings and arrive a few minutes early. (Avoid being the last one rushing into the room.)

- Do not talk over your employees in a meeting.

- Do not talk over your superiors (upper management) in a meeting.

- If your superiors are running a meeting with outside parties, then defer to them to speak for the team/company unless they need or expect your assistance.

- Be respectful to your superiors in addressing them, both in person and in writing.

- Do not talk about or undermine your immediate supervisor or their decisions with your subordinates or peers.

    Try to find someone outside of your organization to discuss that relationship, if needed, so it does not come back on you with inferences of being disloyal. (See Chapter 13, "Be Honest with Yourself and Grow," in the "Who Checks You" section.)

- Maintain a smart appearance.

- Shave before work every day if you are a man.

- Keep your hair looking neat and well-groomed.

  Men: Not too short in length, get it cut every four weeks at a maximum.

  Women: Hair length optional, but consider coloring if stray greying occurs, unless all grey is the look you eventually desire.

  Stay away from the urge to dye your hair with flamboyant colors. This avoids causing a distraction and unnecessary judgements about you and your abilities.

- Replace clothes that are looking worn or faded. (We will talk more about dressing for success in Chapter 15.)

- Iron the clothes that you wear to work.

- Clean and shine your shoes.

- Last but not least, be pleasant and smile often!

Overarching

All of these things may seem small and insignificant by themselves, but when you put them together, they add up to a person who is more about excellence than staying with the rest of the pack. That is the separation factor you want. You will find yourself setting a higher standard, one of excellence, which will morph into your other professional areas and constructively manifest itself in your performance. Your employees and senior management will take notice. With excellence comes trust. Meaning, you will be the person at work called on to lead that one special project or take over a struggling work unit or division. Then you will do it, and do it well. The affirmation and recognition will follow. You can have grand slam moments in your career that are set up by doing the little things to separate yourself from the rest.

CHAPTER 15

DRESS FOR SUCCESS

Whether you like it or not, how you dress says a lot about you and how you want to be regarded by others. Do the clothes make the man (or woman) or does the man (or woman) make the clothes? The answer to that is "yes!" I know we are in a more relaxed society than in years past, but where you are and where you are heading as a professional are synonymous with how you dress the part. Dressing as though you do not care says a lot about you to the observer - including management. Keep in mind that you not only represent yourself but your work unit, department, manager, and company or organization. Yes, there is more to a person than the clothes on their back. However, how you present yourself goes a long way toward influencing the observer about who you are. It can help or hinder your career. In many work environments that have direct customer interaction, how you dress many times shows the other party what you think of them. Your messaging (continuation from Chapter 3, "Don't Lose Your Messaging") to those around you includes who you work for and work with. You want to send a message that you are about excellence and that you are a professional who is worth people's time and serious consideration. You cannot do that wearing flip-flops and jeans no matter how intelligent or capable you really are. Only on a television sitcom or in a Silicon Valley start-up company can you potentially get away with that type of apparel. Do not get me wrong, I enjoy being at home in my comfortable clothes. However, I am not paid to be at home in those clothes. I am paid when I go to work and earn my salary. That requires me to adjust to my company's organizational culture and setting, which includes properly dressing for the type of work I do and the position I hold. This is with or without an established company dress code being enforced. Specifically, the company or organization that employs you has a culture that includes an official or unofficial dress code. Within that dress code, you have to find your comfort zone and make adjustments if need be.

What they should have told you in undergraduate or graduate school is that in the professional arena, you should dress in a manner that endorses your inherent skills and abilities, especially as a manager. You never want to dress in a lesser way that distracts from them. I have seen this happen over and over again with negative consequences. You want to command respect in ALL areas as a manager and one way to do this is to dress appropriately for the work you do. This is your messaging to the observer.

I am including those who work from home on a normal basis in this dress endeavor. Folks in this type of setting have to be careful not to fall into such a relaxed atmosphere over time that their dress code becomes blurred. This becomes noticeable when they are periodically required to interact with the business world and their customers in a face-to-face manner, outside of their home office. You do want to turn off a client with something as rudimentary as your clothing and appearance. The unspoken rule when working from home is to dress below your normal company's work setting, if you are not taking part in teleconferences. If teleconferences are the norm for you during the workday then I suggest you dress as though you were in your company's office space.

Types of Professional Dress Styles

There are arguably four types of professional dress styles. Those styles are: business casual, casual, business formal, and the latest to arrive on the scene is smart casual.

Business Casual

Business casual is the new normal in most companies, so I will begin there. This dress style is appropriate for a work setting that does not require a suit, sports coat, or tie. Let me give you some practical examples.

I work in a corporate headquarters office, which functions in what would be considered a business casual setting. Male managers in our office environment wear dress slacks, khakis, dress shoes, button-down dress shirts and even polo shirts occasionally. A dress shirt with tie is optional during the workweek and some managers wear those. Furthermore, a tie and sports coat is added and definitely fitting when hosting higher-level visitors in a meeting format. For jewelry, a nice wristwatch is worn with either a black or brown leather strap, depending on the color of your clothes. Friday's are considered "casual Fridays" and you will usually find many of us wearing a pair of jeans or khakis, unless higher-level meetings are scheduled.

Many women managers in my corporate headquarters office wear business separates more often than a full pantsuit or skirt suit. They also wear dress slacks with a nice blouse and may add a light waistcoat to their outfit. Their dress shoes range from comfortable flats to pumps in various heights. Residing in southern California allows them to incorporate pumps with an open toe. However, women should shy away from open toed shoes in a professional setting if possible. The jewelry worn is not outlandish but definitely more accentuating to the individual's outfit.

So that is part of my organization's culture of business casual and hence, its expectation of its managers. I still own plenty of suits and ties from working in Washington, D.C. However, I do not like the constricted way a tie makes me feel around the neck. I can wear it but once again, my organization's culture does not require it, so I do not. If that were the expectation, then I would comply. Never be a rebel regarding organizational culture issues such as this. Choose the bigger issues in the workplace if you have to fall on your sword. You should remind yourself that being a manager is a "role" you fill during the workweek. It is not your entire life.

Another one of my life's philosophies is, "Everything in life is a tradeoff." This does not mean that you are a sell-out to who you really are. When you think about it, life consists of a series of tradeoffs to include the requirements of the position you currently encumber or the next one you aspire to attain. If you want to be in management, then you need to set yourself apart and distinguish yourself as a professional. You have to decide to "up your game" or stay where you are at. You cannot go halfway on anything you do especially if you desire to be in management. Dress is one of those areas. Furthermore, you do not want to give the competition, whether internal or external, any opportunity to diminish who you are by evaluating your appearance.

The way you come across infers either your zest for or reluctance to fill the professional role of manager when compared to your peers.

I live and work in San Diego, California. If you surveyed my clothing closet, you will find that about 50% of my wardrobe is work clothing. I normally do not wear any of those clothes on my personal time. It is not because they are not nice clothes. It is simply because that type of clothing does not fit my post nine-to-five style. You will typically find me in a nice pair of shorts and a T-shirt when I am out and about on the weekend enjoying the sunny southern California climate. There are exceptions to that, such as on the occasions that I go to opening night of opera season in which I may break out the tuxedo for my black tie appearance. (I like pulling off the Humphrey Bogart in Casablanca look!) That is definitely not the norm for me but simply my personal style for that particular type of recreational setting.

Casual

It is difficult for me to recognize casual as an official professional dress style, especially for a manager, as society today has taken the term "casual" to another level. Casual dress in the workplace used to mean polo shirts, crew neck sweaters, slacks and jeans (if clearly permitted). There were no faded/ripped jeans or T-shirts allowed. Sneakers were acceptable of course.[1] This concept has changed though, and sometimes not always for the better. Many companies have had to inject their HR department into the mix to craft a policy curbing the ultra-relaxed standard of dress being exhibited by its employees. HR's goal was to ensure some type of standard was instituted that identified boundaries. If your employees are warehouse or dockworkers, then I get it. However, office environments and customer service roles dictate a certain level of attire. Upper management sets the tone and expectations for its employees and defines an organizational culture and setting. That ultimately is what the workforce will follow.

Yet, I acknowledge that certain organizations, tech companies in particular, have a casual dress code that allow their employees to wear jeans and T-shirts to work. I have a good friend who is a talented computer programmer and has worked at tech companies for many years. When I actually saw his wardrobe hanging in the large closet of his very nice suburban home, I was speechless. His wardrobe consisted mostly of T-shirts and blue jeans. That is his world and his organization's culture and setting. However, I do not believe that all of his upper management is wearing exactly the same thing!

If you are a manager in this type of relaxed organizational culture, then try to set yourself apart by dressing just a notch above the rest. How do you do this? Practically speaking, wear denim jeans or khaki pants. Wear collared shirts that are clean and ironed. Wear shoes other than sneakers. Just these little things will separate you from the workforce and your fellow managers. You will know you are doing this well when someone can look at the group of employees you are standing with and clearly say, "That person must be one of the people in charge around here," simply by the way you are dressed. Remember, imaging is important, especially as you are looking for your next promotion.

Business Formal

The business formal dress style is the highest level of professional work dress. Depending on the type of organization or the senior level of your position will clearly define this style. There are obvious reasons for this style to embody an organization. Law firms and financial investment companies will personify the business formal look.[1] No lawyer would show up for court in their smart casual garb for example, as I do not believe the judge would look too highly upon it. Furthermore, the customer who walks into a financial investment company with large sums to invest will think twice if they see poorly dressed financial advisors that are potentially going to serve them. Perception and presentation are important in these business formal companies regardless of how educated or intelligent the employees are. Once again, as a manager you need to understand the organizational culture you are a part of and the respect you want to receive. How you dress many times relays to the other party the respect you are willing to show them. Do not forget this important fact.

The attire for business formal is a suit in what I call the "Washington, D.C. colors," which are black, navy blue, or grey. For men, have your suit tailored to your body size. Do not rely on the off-the-shelf tailored fit as they can make you appear sloppy. Dress shirts in basic colors of mostly white, then blue, and some eggshell are the standard apparel. Cuffs are optional. Non-gaudy ties that are more conservative are typical. Shoes can be oxfords, cap toes, or wing tips. For jewelry, a nice wristwatch is worn with either a black or brown leather strap, depending on the suit color, or a stainless steel watch bracelet. In addition, tasteful lapel pins are optional.

For women, both suit types, pant and skirt, should be utilized. Women have more leeway with the color of blouses but once again, do not let them be too flamboyant as to be a distraction. Also, be careful on how low the blouse is cut in the front. Shoes should be pumps that are closed-toe. Jewelry should be conservative and modestly accentuating the individual's outfit.

Smart Casual

The smart casual dress style is a mixture of the business formal and casual styles for flexible office/informal settings. This look is becoming popular with the younger generation to mix and match the styles of both formal and informal articles of clothing. For men, any combination goes to include suit jackets, sports coats, ties, khakis, chinos, and dress shirts with jeans if desired. However, the one caveat is not to wear dress pants with the outfit.[2] Shoes can run the whole assortment and include oxfords, cap toes, wing tips, monk straps, dress boots, loafers, or sneakers. Socks are optional but it is totally acceptable to throw a pair of cheeky looking ones into your smart casual ensemble, and now you are golden!

For women, any combination goes as well to include blazers, dresses, long skirts, slacks, chinos, and jeans. Just about any kind of nice top can be used such as blouses, button-down shirts, T-shirts, and sweaters. Also, do not forget the scarf as an accessory! Shoes can be heels, flats, or open-toe.

It could be said that the smart casual style exemplifies the new business startup companies that are being founded by the 20-something-year-olds. Many have their own sense of individuality and flare that goes against the traditional business norm. It is sort of the rebel look for the younger generation that knows it still needs to be a part of the professional ranks, but with an edge.

Tips Regardless of Dress Style

The tips below are the basics regardless of what you actually wear. Stay with these norms, and you will be successful.

- Keep your clothes ironed.

- Keep your shoes clean and polished if they are dress shoes.

- Your belts should not be frayed.

- Your shirts, blouses, pants, skirts, dresses, socks, or stockings should not have any rips, holes, look worn out, or be soiled.

- Wear colors that compliment your complexion.

- Be mindful that wearing brown clothing can project a tired look onto your appearance.

- Dress one level above your audience's dress style when making an official presentation.

- Wear the color black if you want to give the perception of looking slimmer or smaller. It is helpful if you have a larger frame.

- Wear the color white if you want to give the perception of looking thicker or larger and more imposing. It can be helpful if you have a smaller frame.

> Fun note: The famous boxer, Sugar Ray Leonard, was a lean athlete who fought mostly as a light welterweight (135 -140 lbs.). Being 5' 9" in height and in that weight class did not produce a very imposing frame. As he became more successful and famous, rumor had it that he would intentionally wear white to his press conferences to give the appearance he was actually bigger in stature than he really was. Very smart!

- Wearing striped shirts or pinstriped suits can make you appear to be heavier than you really are. Keep this in mind if you are stout.

- Keep arm tattoos covered with long-sleeve shirts.

- Keep neck tattoos covered with collared shirts.

For men:

- Do not wear double-breasted suits if you are below 5'10" in height. It can give the appearance that you are shorter.

- Do not wear cuffs on your pants if you are below 5'10" in height. It can give the appearance that you are shorter.

- A necktie will tend to illuminate your face so the color you choose is important.

- Always have a nice pair of black and brown dress shoes in your wardrobe. If anything, you will need it for interviews or weddings!

For women:

- Keep cosmetics basic and conservative.

- Don't over accessorize. Less is better.

- Maintain several pair of black pumps in different heights and styles. Other standard colors of shoes will be needed to match your outfits.

- Flats are good to own, especially if you are taller.

In Summary

Everything that I have mentioned in this chapter is intended to polish you. You have inside of you untapped abilities and potential that only need a chance to be recognized. Give yourself every opportunity to do so by distinguishing yourself by the way you dress. Many times in management as well as in life, it is the little things that set you apart from the rest of the pack. Messaging is also important with those you interact. The way you dress sends a message that you are about excellence when done in a quality and professional manner, regardless of the dress style.

Consequently, it should be noted that your dress style will probably motivate your employees to follow suit. They are observing you, which means you have more influence on them than you may think.

Finally, it is not your dress style or any one thing that makes you a successful manager. It is who you are in totality, made up of the many aspects you possess. I remember watching the celebrity Cher in an interview a few years ago discussing her mother's encouragement she received early in her life before she became famous. Her mother said to her, and I am paraphrasing, "You may not be the best singer, the most beautiful looking, the smartest, the most talented, etc. but when you put it all together (the entire package of who you are), you can be very successful." That is you, too! So dress for success because success is already in you!

CHAPTER 16

LAUGH A LITTLE, THEN LAUGH A LOT

As I look back on my career, I can now smile and laugh about it all - the good, the bad, and yes, even the ugly. We take ourselves so seriously in the pursuit of perfection, intellectually knowing we will never be able to achieve it, but deep down we are emotionally unwilling to accept that truth. Like many, I have poured my time, passion, and sweat equity into many organizations and sometimes wondered if my efforts made a difference. Well, your efforts do make a difference. When in doubt let your overarching theme be to "do good" for your employer and take care of those who work for you. Remember, your job is to make your boss' life easier. In the same manner, hire employees who will make your life easier due to their diligence and being the right fit for your workplace.

What they should have told you in undergraduate or graduate school is that when it is all said and done, you have to be able to laugh. Laugh at yourself, your company, your bosses, your co-workers, and your employees. I am not suggesting you do that in a mean or vindictive way but in a light-hearted and "water off a duck's back" sort of way. All of these entities are going to say and do things that will drive you crazy if you let them. As much as you can, try not to take things personal. It took me a long time to realize and accept this, mainly because of my more serious and intense personality make-up.

I tell my younger employees that when they move on to future positions and ultimately their last professional position, they probably will not look back on their career and remember the projects they worked on or the time spent in traffic getting to and from the office. What they will remember most is the quality relationships they developed with those they worked with and the bosses they worked for. All of the long hours, the late microwave dinners, the work travel stories, the office jokester, the beautiful or handsome looking co-worker you wished you had met years ago, the good boss, the bad boss, the crazy boss, etc. it all runs together in this journey called life that we are fortunate enough to enjoy. So indulge yourself. Laugh a little, and then laugh a lot.

I have tried to help coach you in a practical way with this book as indicated by its title *Management 101: What They Should Have Told You.* I am sure there is a *Management 201* or *Management 301* book out there somewhere, you know, the upper graduate version for senior level managers with corporate takeover aspirations! Mine was but an attempt to relay the wisdom and knowledge that I wished someone in management who was further down the line than I was, would have told me early in my career. It would have made the journey less arduous and allowed me to avoid a few pitfalls as a manager. I have found the real treasure in acquiring knowledge is to share it with others. I have shared with you, and I thank you for reading my book. I hope it helps you as you begin your management career or aspire to the next level of management. Remember, you are better than you think you are and have so much more untapped ability and potential inside just waiting to come out. May your challenging experiences of the past and your well-earned opportunities of the future come together and allow you to emerge victorious. Be well!

About the Author

John Balestrieri was born in western Pennsylvania just outside of Pittsburgh. Raised second generation to Italian immigrants, John was afforded a foundation of hard work, honesty, and respect that forged his character. Beginning his career as an Industrial Engineer with an operations focus facilitated the development of a multidimensional skill set. This resulted in a dexterity to transition into many diverse manager positions over his career while gaining 25+ years of management experience. John is an out-of-the-box thinker who allows his creative and technical sides to converge into innovative problem solving. He possesses extensive and practical leadership experience with a business acumen due to living and managing in multicultural environments and locations. John is a born teacher with a wealth of knowledge and a passion to help those who want to grow, providing professional and personal coaching to assist individuals in achieving their career and life goals.

John received a Bachelor of Science in Industrial Engineering from the University of Pittsburgh and a Master of Business Administration from UCLA. He was the Deputy Financial Director for the United States Navy SEALs at their headquarters in Coronado, CA. Known as a dynamic speaker with an engaging personality, John brings a unique sense of humor and keen wit to any forum providing the audience with a rewarding experience. He is available to speak at your company or organization. Contact John at *jxbenterprises1@gmail.com* for more information.

SOURCES

Chapter 1: Organizational Design

1.   N. (s.d.) Matrix Management and Structure. Accessed December 11, 2019 through https://www.referenceforbusiness.com/encyclopedia/Man-Mix/Matrix-Management-and-Structure.html

2.   N. (s.d.) Max Weber. Accessed December 11, 2019 through http://en.wikipedia.org/wiki/Max_Weber

3.   Mulder, P. (2017). Bureaucratic Theory by Max Weber. Accessed April 5, 2019 through https://www.toolshero.com/management/bureaucratic-theory-weber/

4.   Chand, S. (s.d.) Weber' Bureaucracy: Definition, Features, Benefits, Disadvantages and Problems. Accessed December 11, 2019 through http://www.yourarticlelibrary.com/management/webers-bureaucracy-definition-features-benefits-disadvantages-and-problems/27893

5.   Judge, M. (1999). Office Space. Judgmental Films.

Chapter 5: Understanding Leadership

1. TEC. (2019). 9 common leadership styles: Which type of leader are you? Accessed June 10, 2019 through https://tec.com.au/resource/9-common-leadership-styles-which-type-of-leader-are-you/

2. N., (s.d.) Blood, toil, tears and sweat. Accessed December 10, 2019 through https://en.wikipedia.org/wiki/- Blood,_toil,_tears_and_sweat

Chapter 7: Change Management

1.   Oxford, (s.d.) Definition of Change Management. Accessed July 1, 2019 through https://www.lexico.com/definition/change_management

2.   Sherman, R., Sherman, R. (1964) Mary Poppins Album. (Original Soundtrack). Walt Disney Records.

3.   Coen, J., Coen, E. (2000) O Brother, Where Art Thou. Touchtone Pictures, Universal Pictures, StudioCanal, Working Title Films, Blind Bard Pictures.

4.   Kotter, J. (2012) Leading Change. (1st edition). Harvard Business Review Press.

Chapter 9: Hiring/Staffing

1. Lucas, G., Meyjes, M. (1989) Indiana Jones and the Last Crusade. Lucasfilm Ltd.

Chapter 11: Men and Women Workforce Dynamics

1. Fuhrmans, F. (2019) The First Step Is the Steepest. The Wall Street Journal, 15 October 2019, pp. R1.

2. Fuhrmans, F. (2019) The First Step Is the Steepest. The Wall Street Journal, 15 October 2019, pp. R3.

3. Huang, J, Krivkovich, A, Starikova, I, Yee, L, and Zanoschi, D. (October 2019). Women in the Workplace 2019. Accessed October 23, 2019 through https://www.mckinsey.com/featured-insights/gender-equality/women-in-the-workplace-2019

4. Fontana, F. (2019) Tell It Like It Is. The Wall Street Journal, 15 October 2019, pp. R10.

Chapter 12: Working with or in a Military Culture

1. DarkRiches61. (2018) Rank Insignia of the U.S. Armed Forces. Accessed February 4, 2019 through https://www.reddit.com/r/coolguides/comments/95smiv/us_military_rank_insignia_enlisted_officer

Chapter 13: Be Honest with Yourself and Grow

1. ZGS. Daniel Goleman's five components of emotional intelligence (February 1, 2009). Accessed November 20, 2019 through

    https://web.sonoma.edu/users/s/swijtink/teaching/ philosophy101-/paper1/goleman.htm

2. Management Concepts (2015). Emotionally Intelligent Leadership. (Version: 05-22-15). Management Concepts

Chapter 15: Dress for Success

1. Symington, A. (2016). Workplace Attire: The Difference Between Casual, Business Casual

and Formal. Accessed October 2, 2019 through http://www.charlottparent.com/CLT/Blogs/Manners-Please/Workplace-Attire-The-Difference-Betweeen-Casual-And-Formal

2.   N. (2017). Smart Casual vs Business Casual Attire for Men: What's the Difference? Accessed October 2, 2019 through http://mysocietysocks.com/blogs/news/smart-casual-vs-business-casual-attire-for-men-whats-the-difference

www.ingramcontent.com/pod-product-compliance
Lightning Source LLC
Chambersburg PA
CBHW031219290326
41931CB00035B/410